Pamela German

Capital Dining

Capital Dining

Anne DesBrisay's Guide to Ottawa Restaurants

Published by ECW PRESS
2120 Queen Street East, Suite 200, Toronto, Ontario, Canada M4E 1E2

NATIONAL LIBRARY OF CANADA CATALOGUING IN PUBLICATION DATA

DesBrisay, Anne
Capital dining: Anne DesBrisay's guide to Ottawa restaurants: casual and fine dining in the National Capital Region.

ISBN 1-55022-642-8

1. Restaurants — Ontario — Ottawa — Guidebooks. 2. Restaurants — Quebec — Gatineau — Guidebooks. I. Title.

TX910.C2D37 2004   647.95713'84   C2003-907317-3

Acquisition: Robert Lecker
Editor & production manager: Emma McKay
Cover design, layout & typesetting: Guylaine Regimbald
Ottawa proofreader: Antonia Morton
Printing: Transcontinental

This book is set in Minion and Serlio

The publication of *Capital Dining* has been generously supported by the Canada Council, by the Government of Ontario through the Ontario Media Development Corporation's Ontario Book Initiative, by the Ontario Arts Council, and by the Government of Canada through the Book Publishing Industry Development Program. **Canadä**

Distribution

CANADA
Jaguar Book Group, 100 Armstrong Avenue,
Georgetown, Ontario L7G 5S4

UNITED STATES
Independent Publishers Group, 814 North Franklin Street,
Chicago, Illinois 60610

EUROPE
Turnaround Publisher Services, Unit 3, Olympia Trading Estate,
Coburg Road, Wood Green, London N2Z 6T2

AUSTRALIA AND NEW ZEALAND
Wakefield Press, 1 The Parade West (Box 2266),
Kent Town, South Australia 5071

PRINTED AND BOUND IN CANADA

ECW PRESS
ecwpress.com

For my husband Ken
and
our boys Peter, Sam, Erik, and Thomas

CONTENTS

Listings

ACKNOWLEDGMENTS

My thanks to the ECW Press team—particularly its publisher, Jack David, and my editor, Emma McKay. My thanks as well to Ron Eade, my editor at the *Ottawa Citizen*, and to the readers who write in with suggestions, with support for a review, or with harsh criticism of my criticism. I have learned from all of you.

Thanks to Jane and Saša Petricic, for their good company at many tables. And thanks to Charles Long, Rosaleen Fowler, Kate Genest, Catherine Tighe, Beryle Girard, and Carol Upton for their thorough and generous help. Above all, I would like to thank Ken, who gave more than any husband should. In addition to letting me help myself to the contents of every plate ever put in front of him, he took charge of the owl projects and hockey practices while I was dining out.

INTRODUCTION

Just over ten years ago, the first restaurant I visited as food critic for the *Ottawa Citizen* was a legendary institution called The Green Valley. I remember a certain British structure to the meal: tomato juice, iceberg lettuce with radish, a New York steak with potatoes and peas, and a wedge of coconut cream pie. Looked a lot like my childhood. Very white-bread, very Toronto. *Very* 1960s.

A restaurant or two later, more white bread. A pancake actually, about the size of a dinner plate but delivered draped in layers over a large tin tray, its pale spongy surface covered with dollops of earth-coloured stews of varying intensities. This was injera, fashioned from an Ethiopian grain called teff, and we tore off pieces to scoop dollops into our mouths. A new "white bread" for Ottawa; a new cuisine for me.

This job has taken me to fabulous places—Spain, Vietnam, Thailand, Italy and all its regions, Japan, France (and France and France), Texas, Jamaica, Mexico, and Somalia. It has also brought me home: to the food in my backyard, to the beauty of a roasted parsnip, a bowl of wild blueberries, a luscious slice of smoked Atlantic salmon.

Some might say that the mark of a world-class city is having superb restaurants that get written up in travel magazines and win international awards for their wine lists. If that's true, then Ottawa-Gatineau has arrived, and then some. And that's a great thing. But what delights me just as much is the rise I've witnessed in the standards of that mass of mid-priced restaurants—the neighbourhood bistros, cafés, and pubs that now pepper this region. These accessible, affordable, come-as-you-be eateries are now catering to more educated diners: you and me. We're the ones who collect cookbooks, buy foodie magazines, attend the occasional cooking class at our local supermarket, and watch hours of celebrity cooking shows on TV. We know about homemade stock and free-range chickens and how to make a decent risotto. And restaurants know that we know. And that too is a great thing.

In this book, you'll find those wonderful award-winning restaurants that are putting the National Capital Region on the gastronomic map. You'll also find the neighbourhood café with the smoky black-bean soup, and the local Thai bistro with a to-die-for pad Thai.

This book is a compilation of restaurants I feel I can recommend —some unequivocally, others with some reservations. It does not represent a definitive or exhaustive list. What it does represent is an honest, objective reflection of my experiences.

I choose the restaurants that I visit; no one sends me. I behave myself. I do not draw attention to my table. I review anonymously, making reservations under assumed names. Anonymity means I receive from the serving staff and the kitchen the same treatment (the same injera, the same peas) that you do. I guard my identity fiercely, and in twelve years of critiquing restaurants, I've managed to be able to walk into any one of them as just the ordinary, hungry, thirsty gal at table seven.

The other thing you need to remember as you read this collection is that restaurants open, restaurants close, and restaurants change hands, chefs, servers, identities—even wall colourings—at alarming rates. I offer this book as a guide. It is not a guarantee of what you will find. But I hope it will help you on your own search.

Book a table. Raise a glass. Good eating!

HOW TO USE THIS BOOK

The Star Ratings

★★   Good and reliable
★★★   Very good
★★★★   Excellent, one of the region's best

The Dollar Signs

$ Modestly priced: under $40
$$ Moderately priced: $40-$70
$$$ Expensive: $70-$100
$$$$ Very expensive: Over $100

Each price classification is based on the cost of a typical dinner for two people: starter, main dish, dessert, coffee, taxes, and a 15% gratuity. The bill does not include any wine or drinks.

A Note on Smoking
There is no smoking in any restaurant in Ottawa, though you may smoke on some outdoor patios. At press time, most restaurants across the bridges, in Gatineau, still have smoking sections. Best to ask when making a reservation.

A Note on Dialing
Many North American cities now use ten-digit phone numbers. Ottawa is not yet one of them. If you're in Ottawa-Gatineau, simply dial the seven digits. If you're calling from outside the National Capital Region, use the area code.

ALLEGRO

★★½   Italian $$$

Today's Italian ristorante is more likely to be a modish room of cutting-edge design than anything resembling the dusky-lit, red-check-tablecloth, candle-in-a-Chianti eatery of yore. But for all its remodelled interiors, the menu you remember from 1984 is likely the same one you'll get in 2004.

For the most part, Italian dining rooms serve the same traditional red-sauced dishes you've always seen; same carrot-broccoli accompaniments; same tomato-basil salad on a January menu as on a September one.

Still, for all my grumbling about static, photo-fit menus, my romance with Italian standards—a pungent puttanesca, a full-bodied straciatella, a melting veal saltimbocca—endures.

And these standards are well executed at Allegro, a small, handsome dining room of fifteen tables, considerately served.

Great soups here: tortellini, with delicate veal-stuffed pasta pouches submerged in a full-bodied chicken stock; or a fall soup of butternut squash, pretty with swirls of roasted red pepper purée.

Carpaccio is carved to order, the meltingly good ruby meat sharpened with strong parmigiano livened with lemon and pepper. A starter of eggplant, thinly sliced, is filled with a blend of ricotta and parmigiano cheeses, baked to just-yielding and doused in a lively tomato sauce. Homemade sausages are well-flavoured, piquant, jazzed up with banana peppers and black olives.

The broccoli-carrot ordeal is not part of the Allegro package. Accompanying the veal chop (fat, succulent, only somewhat over-grilled) and the featured trout (impeccable) are roasted potatoes, peppers, eggplant, zucchini, and squash, all faultless. They do a good job with fish here. Sea bass is cooked until the flesh releases the bone and not a second longer; then lightly napped with a wine and parsley sauce, and generously mounted with butter.

Allegro's risottos have never let me down. Arborio rice is coddled to toothsome perfection and crowned with seafood: mussels, shrimp, and scallops.

Desserts are the standards: tartufo, crème caramel, zabaglione, cheesecake flavoured with some liqueur or other, and tiramisu (of course) — this version fresh, boozy, and strong of strong coffee flavour.

There is a regular wine list — one page, all Italian — and a much bigger vintage selection of mostly Italian bottles.

ALLEGRO
422 Preston St. (at Beech)
(613) 235-7454
www.allegroristorante.ca
Access: Steps into restaurant; washrooms are upstairs
Price: Pasta, risotto, and main dishes $10.95 to $39.95
Open: Lunch Mon.-Fri.; dinner daily

AMBER GARDEN

★★   **Eastern/Central European** $$

Arrive hungry for an Amber Garden dinner. You will eat weightily on dishes "dedicated to the culinary traditions of the people on the ancient European Amber Route."

From the whimsically hand-painted wall-size map in the Garden's foyer, you get your first hint that you will eat food deriving from the Baltic Sea to the Mediterranean. And while it's not particularly subtle or complicated fare, it is absolutely tasty and comforting.

You must, of course, have borscht. Amber Garden's version is lighter than you'd expect, but with no shortage of beet flavour. We are happy for the chopped mushrooms within the warm goose liver pâté, for the coarse, highly seasoned wedge has a robust livery flavour the 'shrooms manage to ease.

The salads are vegetarian meals all on their own. Both the Polish and the Russian salads are large, attractively presented mounds of freshly chopped vegetables and well-seasoned mayonnaise. Beets in the Russian salad turn the crunchy mound pink. Skip the bits and pieces around the perimeter of the plate, though — triangles of tasteless marble cheese and pale pink November tomatoes add nothing but volume to a plate that's already bulging.

There are three bird dishes, two ways with fish, and some meatless pierogies, but — let's not fool ourselves here — meat dominates the mains. The Amber platter (served for one, but could feed four) allows you to graze through house specialties like kniedlicky, highly seasoned dumplings that come with seriously rich mashed potatoes and a mélange of turnip, carrot, and red pepper. The cabbage rolls are stuffed with beef and rice, balanced with a good tomato sauce. The pierogies — both the meat-filled and the cheese-and potato-filled versions—are light, almost delicate, laced with slow-cooked onion and served with full-fat sour cream.

There is chicken—juicy and potently spiced with paprika—and there are superior sausages, lean, spicy, full-flavoured. Beef rouladen is somewhat dry, but has a very tasty stuffing. And finally, the goulash is seductively wrapped in an enormous latke, or potato pancake.

Desserts here are not an afterthought. The plum cake is exceptional; ditto the crêpes (filled with sweet cheese and covered with a good chocolate sauce) and the chocolate walnut torte (very fresh, more nutty than sweet). The Russian tea will keep you awake all night.

AMBER GARDEN
1 & 3 Richmond Rd. (one block east of Island Park)
(613) 725-2757
www.ambergarden.net
Access: Fully accessible
Price: Main dishes $13.95 to $24.95
Open: Lunch Tues.-Fri.; dinner Tues.-Sat.; closed Sun. & Mon.

ANNA

★ ★ ½   Thai $$

Of all the various Thai restaurants Art Akarapanich has launched in Ottawa over the past twenty-five years, Anna stands out.

For one, she's the prettiest. In a city where Asian eating is often relegated to a poster-covered hole-in-the-wall, Anna impresses with rich mustard-coloured walls and luxurious Thai décor blended with funky contemporary furnishings.

You will do well to begin with soup, where the wonder is in the blending of flavours: the citric thrill of lime leaves, the spicy heat of chillies, the sour charge of fish sauce. Some bowls are silky with coconut milk (tom kha kai). Others, like the tom yum goong, are left clear; evidence of a good, fragrant stock is also clear.

There is good saté here, the meat well marinated and char-grilled until tender; the peanut sauce is an indispensable pleasure. Anna's salads pack a plate with flavour — particularly good is the yum ma-muang, based on green mangoes shredded and tossed with shrimp, garlic, coriander, mint, red pepper strips, and peanuts.

Anna's pad Thai is short on sugar and long on charm. Fillets of fried tilapia are bolstered with shredded lime leaves, fine rings of lemongrass and scallion, chopped Thai basil, and fiery red chillies. Duck is steamed, meaty, and moist, fragrant with ginger and accompanied by crunchy green broccoli. Anna's "jungle curry" is a searingly hot dish that manages, despite the litter of chillies, to convey all the subtle flavours of a good Thai curry.

Mango ice cream is a luscious palate-soother, the flavour boosted further with an intense mango coulis. If you're a fan of the classic and can't get enough mango, you'll like Anna's version of sticky rice with mango: the fruit is ripe and the rice has been cooked with just the right amount of coconut milk and sugar, sprinkled with toasted sesame seeds.

Best to drink beer or lemongrass tea with this food.

ANNA
91 Holland Ave. (between Wellington and Scott)
(613) 759-8472
www.thaitaste.ca
Access: Stairs into restaurant; washrooms are upstairs
Price: Main dishes $9.25 to $14.95
Open: Lunch Mon.-Fri.; dinner daily

ARC LOUNGE

★★★ ½   **Contemporary – Canadian** $$$

Up one level from the bare-bones front foyer of the sleek ARC the (dot) Hotel is its restaurant, called the ARC Lounge, fittingly decked out in minimalist style. A long, thin room, the Lounge is divided into areas for its various functions — eating, snacking, drinking, hanging out — with nouveau-retro furniture as section dividers. The lighting is à la mode; the tables are black and bare, save for a white tea light and one carefully placed green apple.

ARC's new chef is Paul Stewart, a Stratford Chefs School graduate who comes here by way of Strewn Winery's restaurant in Niagara. An August amuse-bouche is an impressive first glimpse of Stewart's style: a newborn zucchini, its blossom still on the vine, is halved, hollowed slightly, then built up with fragrant ground lamb, a dollop of tomato relish, and dribbles of fennel oil. Delightful.

Stewart smokes salmon with apple wood, serves it in thick meaty chunks with salads: a baby Yukon Gold, some fruitily dressed greens, and an inspired hummus fashioned with green fresh peas. He presents Malpeque oysters on a bed of rock salt and serves them with a Thai-inspired sauce of red chillies, tomato, garlic, fresh basil, and lime juice. A classic carrot-orange soup has fantastic flavour, and green swirls of fennel oil pattern its surface. A black seaweed salad, pungent with garlic, lime, and sesame oil, sporting a tiny dice of carrot for colour and crunch, provides the bed for four fat shrimp, meaty, sweet, and perfectly grilled.

Main dishes also shine: a grilled Alberta tenderloin is vibrant with flavour, served with roasted onion rings, crisp, well-peppered frites, yellow and green zucchini, and patty pan squash. We order the halibut to get the beets — rings of baby goldens from local organic farmers. We are rewarded with luscious fish, buttery, meltingly good, laid on a bed of al dente barley with licorice rings of fennel. Best not to skip "mom's sweet chilli sauce," as "mom" is Anita Stewart, Canadian food champion, author, and founder of Cuisine Canada. Her boys join a duck's leg (a first-class confit) with garlicky, oil-slicked fava beans and her fragrant, well-balanced sauce. (Mom might tell them, though, that the flourish of puff pastry is hardly necessary.)

Strong too is the all-Canadian cheese menu. A six-year-old unpasteurized cheddar is served with hunks of bitter chocolate; a Québec blue comes with poached pears and roasted walnuts. We accept a glass of port suggested by sommelier Brad Stewart, who attends to our table with an infectious enthusiasm for his brother's food — and for the wine list he's assembled to complement it.

If you like lemon (and I mean LEMON), you'll like the mouth-puckering, exceptionally lemony tart. It hurts my eyes. The traditional Sachertorte is rich chocolate cake, apricot jam spread in the centre, a smooth, bittersweet glaze on top, boozy apricots and candied pecans alongside. The winner, though, is an apple cake, prepared tarte Tatin–style, baked and flipped, with the wedges of Granny Smith a golden caramelized crown. A bittersweet caramel sauce and good cinnamon ice cream finish the plate.

ARC LOUNGE
ARC The.Hotel
140 Slater St. (between O'Connor and Metcalfe)
(613) 238-2888
www.arcthehotel.com
ACCESS: Stairs to front door, more into restaurant
PRICE: Main dishes $18 to $36
OPEN: Breakfast daily; lunch Mon.-Fri.; dinner Mon.-Sat.

AZTECA

★ ★ ½   Mexican $$

A year ago, Azteca was a cafeteria-style hole-in-the-wall of six tables, sixteen chairs, and a bench, mostly filled with Mexican-Canadians looking for the tastes and smells of their homeland.

Re-opened after a massive renovation, Azteca now seats about eighty, on street level and in two rooms upstairs. All traces of its self-service linoleum days have vanished. You enter to a sand-coloured ceramic floor, inlayed with vibrant sections of Mexican tile. The tables are two tones of polished wood. The walls are coffee-cream and Aztec blue, woven in and around the original limestone and brick of the Byward Market.

This is a Mexican restaurant, not Tex-Mex, not chain-Mex; completely fajita-free. It's run by Rosa Acal and her family, originally from Mexico City. They've hired a crew of young servers who speak with pride and intelligence about Chef Juan Carlos' menu: quesadillas, tostadas, enchiladas, tortas, tacos, chiles rellenos.

If your experience with Mexican cooking extends only as far as the local Tex-Mex, you'll find Azteca's tortillas striking. Made to order, fashioned from masa harina (flour ground from corn) and lime water, they're ready to be pressed, shaped, steamed, fried, stuffed, or topped. Sliced, they crown the house sopa, a fairly mild tomato soup fashioned with habañero chillies and moist strips of chicken, topped with avocado, sour cream, and Azteca's tangy queso fresco. You can add one of the three house salsas offered to perk it up: mild, medium, or fiery. The same tacos are used to produce the quesadillas, filled with long strips of moist shredded beef in a modestly spicy fruity tomato sauce.

A mole of medium heat and maximum flavour naps a tortilla-draped, cheese-stuffed poblano pepper, perfectly softened. Strips of marinated pork (pastor) are sharp-flavoured but tender-natured. They arrive with grilled onions and peppers spread on soft corn tortillas, crowned with strips of ripe avocado, tomato, sour cream, and fresh cheese. If you want it livelier, ladle on the salsas. The one with the brownish hue is best drizzled on delicately: full of smoked chipotle chillies, it has big-time punch.

A grainy black mole is an option with the house enchiladas. Created with all the complex ingredients used for many of Mexico's sauces, it is pungent, sour, spicy, and ever so slightly sweet. The chocolate may be what stands out as you taste this mole, but as a gradual heat builds up in your mouth, you are reminded that chilli peppers still play the starring role. On one visit, the shredded chicken inside the tortilla is perfect. Another time, it's dry and juiceless. Pick the right night.

We began with a margarita and then drank Sol beer with this food.

AZTECA
41 William St. (at George)
(613) 241-6050
Access: One step to street-level dining; most of the restaurant is upstairs, as are the washrooms
Price: Main dishes $10 to $22
Open: Daily for lunch and dinner

BECKTA

★★★★   **Contemporary** $$$$

Beckta has embraced what I was beginning to despair of as an outmoded notion. I refer to good service.

This is a thoroughly modern restaurant of eclectic leanings, run by a bunch of youngsters who just "get it." They understand about balancing professional service with genuine hospitality—beginning with how reservations are handled, followed by the greeting given when you arrive, and carried out in the appropriate and unrelentingly courteous attention paid to your table, right through to the bill. It is in this arena that Beckta shines.

The owner, Stephen Beckta, is constantly present—welcoming guests, chatting with them, changing their linen, grinning at staff. At dinner, he talks wine, enthusing about a recently acquired Syrah like a boy talking about a new toy. He infuses the place with his high spirits.

Spirits, you see, are his thing. Beckta is an Algonquin College–trained sommelier who honed his skills in top New York restaurants. He even managed to charm the *New York Times* with his skill and youth. ("Hey, is that sommelier old enough to drink?") And now, not yet thirty years old, he has settled back home, married his Ottawa sweetheart, and (in the space formerly occupied by the Ritz Uptown) opened his self-titled restaurant.

He's hired a capable crew: an entourage of blue-shirted servers who manage both to match the colour of the walls and to perform their duties at impressive levels. Despite my cruellest grilling on the nuances of the menu, there is no stumping them. They have tasted this food, are clearly interested, and are thoroughly briefed. For the frequent diner, it's a rare pleasure.

But the professionalism on the Beckta floor is just half the joy of this place.

The other half is the cooking.

The scampering shadows we see behind an opaque rice paper window are those of twenty-four-year-old chef Stephen Vardy, late of Kinki on York Street, and his team. A Vardy dinner starts with a nano-portioned delicacy. Our night brought smoked scallops dotted with a spicy zucchini relish, presented on Chinese soup spoons. The house breads are good. The browned butter improves them. The "new" chowder gives an Asian twist to a New England classic: fresh clams, fat mussels, and chunks of lardon, leek, and potato drenched in a broth rich with coconut milk and bright with galangal. Perfect gnocchi are ambrosial under tarragon-scented escargots. A so-called teenage salad is indeed a bit nutty, and possessed of some attitude (but not the least bit sullen or immature). It's a mound of bouncy, flavourful leaves of mixed colours and tastes, threaded with deep-fried leek, chives, and moistened with a mirin-based vinaigrette.

The scallops are as good as they get, their surfaces caramelized, milky soft within, anchored on a pile of puréed cauliflower treated with truffle oil and paired with grilled kumquats, caperberries, and local asparagus. And on it goes: grilled peaches and shiitake mushrooms link up with luscious duck. Black olives, roasted ramps, and soft shreds of spätzle complete the lamb. Chicken, wing bone on, breastbone off, is slow roasted to crispy-skin, molten-middle perfection. Star anise flavours the purée of sweet potato on which it is set. Fiddleheads, wild mushrooms, and a vaguely grown-up version of Tater Tots (the chef, recall, is only twenty-four) finish the plate.

A dessert tray full of liberties taken with bananas is a tray full of fun: chocolate banana pudding, banana bread, banana torched, banana gelato, banana compote. . . . Nuttier, but less nuts: a divine chocolate tart with pistachio gelato. And, quite seriously: crème brûlée infused with cardamom and ginger.

The cheeses are ripe; many are local. A glass of port improves them.

The extensive Beckta wine list is an evolving document, with a price structure that seems respectful. There are some "special" wines, certainly, but most are wines I can safely bill the *Citizen*. A quarter of the list is Canadian, and a page is devoted to wines, including sparkling wines, available by the Riedel glass in either a 3 oz or a 6 oz size.

BECKTA
226 Nepean St. (between Kent and Bank)
(613) 238-7063
www.beckta.com
Access: Steps to front entrance; washrooms are upstairs
Price: Main dishes $25 to $34
Open: Lunch Mon.-Fri.; dinner Mon.-Sat.; closed Sun.

BEIJING TIANRUN

★★   Chinese $

Beijing Tianrun is a yellow-walled, brightly lit series of square rooms with a bare-necessities feel to them. The largest room is packed with tables, some square, some round, suitable for extended family dining or banquets. The second and third rooms are smaller, available for private functions or overflow.

There is no overflow at lunch. But at Sunday dinner, all rooms are packed.

Inquiries made in Chinese at neighbouring tables seem to yield more interesting dishes. Our questions (in English) about the extensive menu are clearly beyond our server. Next to us, they appear to be eating beyond the regular menu, or perhaps enjoying those special dishes my children shriek at: shredded jellyfish with sesame, pig's ears in red sauce, stir-fried pig's stomach. I can't report on the ears, hocks, or tummy dishes; but what we ate, we liked.

You order by number. I draw your attention to #1, #25, and #89, our starter courses. The first was a hot-and-sour soup of good hot and sour balance, the viscous broth threaded with silky tofu, bamboo shoots, and mushrooms. The beef pot stickers are bundles of well-seasoned ground meat fried to glistening golden brown in their wonton packages. Spring rolls are deep-fried bundles of flavour: part crunchy, part soft, all addictive.

Moo she pork is sweet, juicy meat, caramelized onions, and soft pancakes, bundled and dunked in hoisin sauce. Roasted duck is cut into slabs of moist meat and crisp skin, weighty with flavour. Crunchy fried egg noodles crown a well-garlicked bowl in which the tangles of noodle are part crispy, part al dente, part soft. In among them are rounds of Chinese mushrooms, slices of pepper, onion, and Chinese greens—all the elements of good flavour.

The sizzling chicken in black bean sauce (#46) is a large portion of juicy chicken under strands of onion, celery, slivers of garlic, and flecks of hot red chillies, in a broth that's thick with the strong, pleasantly gritty beans. Yu Hsing eggplant (#74) joins the oiled Chinese vegetable with peppers in a pungent, sweet, extraordinarily spicy sauce.

The letdown at lunch is the shrimp stir-fry, which suffers from an excess of salt that no amount of rice could counter.

BEIJING TIANRUN
1947 Bank St. (south of Walkley)
(613) 521-3868
Access: Steps into restaurant
Price: Main dishes $6.95 to $18
Open: Daily for lunch and dinner

BÉLAIR SUR LA RIVIÈRE

★★★   French – Canadian $$$

This former home of a Wakefield pizzeria is a small, plain, rather cramped rectangle of a room. At the wrong time of the year, a blast of arctic air swirls in when the front door opens. The heat is cranked up to compensate. Half the restaurant is kitchen: open, accessible, filled with the smells and sounds and all the banged-up pots of a hard-working cookery. A refrigerated counter sells pâtés and desserts, soups and sauces. A bookcase displays organic coffees and jams.

And in the small space that's left, there are five wooden tables at which fourteen fortunates may gather to feast on wonderful food.

Alain Bélair is a graduate of the Stratford Chefs School. He opened Bélair sur la rivière in the summer of 2002, acquired a liquor licence and a wife in the fall, and is now serving lunch and dinner Thursday, Friday, and Saturday nights.

After a few weeks of dining in big-moneyed, designed-up restaurants, it was something of a relief to find myself in this simple little place, chowing down on venison stew with mashed potatoes on a five-and-dime-store dinner plate. And after two tastes of Bélair's cooking, I'm quite prepared to chow down on anything he chooses to put on any plate—the Limoges china of his future, or the current Corningware collection.

Lunch begins with a sweet, deeply flavourful purée of carrot, considerably spiked with chipotle peppers. This is followed by a "caviar" of grill-roasted aubergine, speckled with its black seeds, potent with sultry, smoky flavour. The soft, sloshy interior is mashed with yogurt, a homemade mayonnaise, garlic, and spices, dotted with bits of roasted pepper, and served with grilled potato bread. Glorious. A main-dish spinach salad is dotted with ripe tomatoes, soft cubes of roasted seasoned potatoes, a sauté of wild mushrooms, and moist, rich shreds of duck confit. A red onion tart is prepared tarte Tatin–style, baked and flipped to reveal a top layer of caramelized onion, heady of balsamic vinegar, with a centre of succulent chèvre beneath.

A purée of "sunchoke" (a.k.a. Jerusalem artichoke) has a compellingly nutty, slightly bitter flavour. It's fleshed out with sweet onion and celeriac, and mounted with butter. It begins a Bélair dinner, along with a jelly-crowned crock of chicken liver pâté, boozy with cognac, rich with cream, served with a rhubarb-raisin chutney and more of that dark-crusted potato bread.

Bélair roasts a fat chunk of cod and serves it with a rich butter sauce charged with lemon. Surrounding the fish is a rustic sauté of spinach, red onion, potatoes, and golden beets. And then that venison stew: lean cubes of resilient meat, combined with well-roasted root vegetables, in a vigorously gamey sauce, the whole soaked up with garlicky mashed potatoes.

Desserts are all winners: an intensely lemony tart with a caramelized surface, a silken crème brûlée, or a baked-to-order pear tart on puff pastry, with cream.

The wines offered are few, designed to match the dishes, and all are available by the glass.

BÉLAIR SUR LA RIVIÈRE
759, ch. Riverside (at Mill Rd.)
Wakefield
(819) 459-1445
Access: Two steps at entrance; washrooms are small
Price: Main dishes $18 to $32
Open: Lunch and dinner, Thurs.-Sat.

BELLA'S BISTRO

★★★   Italian $$

When I'm fed up with fashionable food, with decoding the cunning menus of hot new eateries, I head to Bella's. Housed in an elegant brick home bordered by gas stations and convenience stores, this Westboro restaurant is a neighbourhood favourite. Other than the chore of finding a table, nothing about it is unnerving.

What Bella Milito's bistro offers is comfort and consistency: of familiar offerings on a largely unchanging menu, of a staff that knows its business, and yes, of a bill that remains remarkably reasonable. It's an attractive combination, and a successful one. Make a reservation or risk the discomfort of being turned away.

Begin with the mussels. They are served a couple of ways: in a tomato-basil sauce frisky with red chillies and sweetened with roasted garlic, or in a gentler bath of garlic, leeks, wine, and cream. Either way, they're top-notch. The carpaccio too is first-class, the raw, ruby meat slices anchored with a light mustard-brandy sauce, the plate scattered with capers and Parmesan.

Great attention is paid to the pasta at Bella's. The noodles are fresh, precisely cooked, the associated sauces rich with flavour and often with cream. If you wish to avoid a luscious rendezvous with butterfat, opt for noodles pampered with Bella's lively tomato sauce. If you want "as rich as it gets," order the lobster ravioli: sweet with a gentle oceanic flavour, these firm pasta packages are bathed in a cream sauce fragrant with saffron and tarragon.

Long strands of fettuccini, herbed and oiled, combined with garlic, pine nuts, and Parmesan, make a simple, satisfying dish. The house linguine with seafood is a classic: fresh fish married with fresh noodles, united in a spicy tomato sauce piqued with balsamic vinegar. Perhaps the most soothing pasta on the menu is the gnocchi. These potato dumplings are generally lumped into the pasta section, and generally disappoint with leadenness. Here they're exquisite—soft, meltingly good, served either with a fragrant Bolognese sauce or with that cream, garlic, and Parmesan sauce we've encountered and liked here before.

You can make a happy and very affordable meal here with one of Bella's big salads and a plate of pasta. If you'd rather have meat, the veal is reliably tender, served with properly cooked vegetables and roast potatoes. My favourite is the scaloppini de Vitelo Saporite, in a sauce pungent with artichoke hearts, capers, mushrooms, prosciutto, and olives.

You may finish decadently with the chocolate sabayon cake, always a winner, or with a good nutty gelato.

The staff is always knowledgeable about the food and the wine list, and provides a level of professionalism generally reserved for more expensive joints.

BELLA'S BISTRO
45 Richmond Rd. (at Island Park)
(613) 724-6439
www.bellas.ca
Access: Steps into restaurant; washrooms are upstairs
Price: Main dishes $14.95 to $28.95
Open: Lunch Tues.-Fri.; dinner Tues.-Sun.; closed Mon.

BENTO SUSHI

★★   **Japanese** $

Its décor is all but nonexistent. It has no liquor license. It offers nothing hot other than green tea and from-a-package miso soup. And it can accommodate fourteen lucky people at five little tables — the rest of you have to settle for take-away.

What you *will* find in this tiny, modest eatery (once you do find it, for Bento's is set well back from Rideau) is a very fresh-tasting product. And when you're talking fish — and we are here — that's all that really matters. Except, of course, for the skill of the "itamae-san" — that matters too. He's the guy (and they're all guys) who cuts, moulds, and assembles the fish. At Bento, there is considerable skill at work.

By definition, sushi means pretty much anything served with vinegared rice. Bento Sushi offers the standard raw fish varieties — salmon, tuna, snapper, crab (fake, of course), shrimp, yellowtail, some smoked fish (like mackerel and eel) — all sculpted with rice that's just the right degree of sticky, and perked up considerably with a dollop of wasabi. You may garnish the assembly with a whisper or a mountain of rousing pink pickled ginger, dip it or dunk it in a puddle of black soy sauce further livened (or not) with more wasabi, and just pop the whole of that fresh-flavoured construction in your mouth in one yummy fell swoop.

You either relish the complexity of flavours and textures (the crunch of cucumber, the softness of avocado, and the sweet-sour rice, coated with sesame seeds or crackling sheets of seaweed) or savour the utter cleanness of a shimmeringly naked hunk of raw salmon.

If you're looking for tempura, teriyaki, or tonkatsu, best to look elsewhere. Only the raw goods are served here.

If this high-protein, low-fat snack food is your cup of dashi and if you don't want to spend the better part of your take-home pay on it, Bento is an affordable, no-nonsense way to get a sushi fix.

BENTO SUSHI
606 Rideau St. (east of Charlotte)
(613) 562-2563
Access: Fully accessible
Price: Main dishes $5 to $15
Open: Lunch and dinner Mon.-Sat.; closed Sun.

BISTRO 1908

★ ★ ½   French – Bistro $$$

1908 is a hip bistro, housed in a handsome brick building—a great high-ceilinged vault of a place, with pale pine floors and warm chocolate-brown wood. A row of tall spotlights somehow lowers the ceiling, as does the collection of explosive canvasses on the red brick walls. You enter to a bar and smoking section. Down a half-dozen stairs, another forty tables are set with white linen and white paper toppers. At the far end, the open kitchen provides the focal point. A large blackboard above the kitchen window lists the day's specials.

At lunch, this bistro teems with conversation. Occasionally, clouds of smoke drift down from the upper level on to those seated closest to the bar. We ask to move. Our request is graciously accommodated.

On the fall menu: ris de veau, cassoulet, steak tartare, bavette de boeuf with shallot confit, and shrimp with coconut milk, mango chutney, and chipotle peppers.

Circle the one that doesn't belong. And then remember not to order it. 1908 serves good, market-driven, bistro-French food . . . until it strays into Asian territory. (It didn't help that the shrimp were overcooked, but it was the sauce that lacked finesse.)

Better the uncomplicated offerings, which can be brilliant. A cream of vegetable soup has a sweet potato base and colour and much vegetable flavour. The utterly fresh salad leaves are united with a pungent mustard vinaigrette that tastes of Paris cafés. Sweetbreads are crisped in the pan, soft inside, sweetened with a sauce of cider-deglazed pan juices, treated with thyme and honey.

There are gnocchi on the one-page lunch menu, always a good test of a kitchen: these potato dumplings are soft enough, but their warm ratatouille treatment is in need of a flavour boost — some salt, some cheese, more herbs. A large puddle of sauce beside a brochette of exquisite tuna (buttressed with cherry tomato and red onion) looks alarmingly like Kraft Catalina, but tastes like nothing of the kind. This is a roasted red pepper and passion fruit dressing with lots of pleasurable zing.

At dinner, the salmon is baked to perfection, crusted with mustard. Alongside there is a piquant horseradish cream sauce and some well-cooked vegetables: "broccoflower," carrot, turnip, braised baby bok choy. A neighbouring table has ordered the steak-frites, and the fries scream out to us. Our server doesn't bat an eye when we order a plate to share. He's used to this. The deep-fried potatoes are sweet, crisp, soft inside and thyme-flecked, served with mayonnaise. One order is hardly enough.

For dessert, profiteroles, bien sûr, and a pecan tart that's about the best I've ever tasted.

The wine list is long and varied, and offers many choices by the glass.

BISTRO 1908
70, Promenade du Portage (at Leduc)
Gatineau (Hull district)
(819) 770-1908
Access: Easy access to top level (smoking section); washrooms are accessible
Price: Main dishes $17.75 to $23.75
Open: Lunch Mon.-Fri.; dinner Mon.-Sat.; closed Sun.

BLACK CAT CAFÉ

★★★ ½   **Contemporary**   **$$$**

For a good many years before it moved to its current quarters in the Byward Market, the Black Cat was a happening café on Echo Drive. That was back when there wasn't a great deal else of interest on the restaurant scene.

The Black Cat is owned and operated, then as now, by Richard Urquhart, who is much around and much the spirit of the place.

The Murray Street digs are understated: lights are halogen, walls are tamarind, tables are bare, art is bold, and clutter is nowhere. An enclosed non-smoking patio at the back beckons diners in the more gentle seasons. There is one exception to these otherwise tranquil furnishings: the TVs in the washrooms come complete with remote control. My husband has been known (on game nights, say) to excuse himself a while. I've managed to resist their appeal, never finding they could compete with the food—which seems better to me every visit.

My first taste was in its first year, when this café was called the Black Cat Wine and Noodle Bar. In those early days, food mostly came in wide, shallow bowls, with Asian noodles providing the foundation for the various things that settled on top and pooled beneath. Chopsticks and Chinese soup spoons were provided along with the knives and forks.

No longer. The menu still has Asian influences (what contemporary menu doesn't?) but the food seems designed less to be tricky or thematic than to simply taste good.

Mussels, shrimp, scallops, and salmon are faultless in a tomato-reddened broth supported with crisp julienne vegetables. The char-edged squid starter is one of the most tender versions you'll ever encounter, served atop a mound of wilted watercress strewn with sweetly grilled tomatoes and black olives.

Quail is a tasty wee bird, boned, flattened, grilled to tender and served with a mustard-dressed warm potato salad dotted with smoky bacon. Luscious shrimp are lightly touched with curry, paired with risotto fashioned into a cake, and moistened with a lemony beurre blanc.

Main courses are led by duck, fabulous for its contrasts: the crisp, amber skin, the tender, deeply-smoked flesh, and the sweet and crackling shreds of fried leek strewn on top. Fat slabs of pork tenderloin are pink and moist, their rims crusted and fired up with a good jerk rub. Game is well managed: venison is rosy red, the hefty slices set on a foundation of wilted bitter greens, topped with a deep-fried tangle of carrot, potato, and leek and rimmed with a dark, beer-rich sauce. Fish too: a meaty marlin is sushi-rare inside, attractively grill-marked, sweetly balanced with a grilled pineapple salsa. On the side, a cabbage salad doused with rice vinegar and sesame oil. About the only letdown among the mains is a bland roasted vegetable strudel.

The pear tarte Tatin is a knockout. The fragrant Bosc pears are treated with a white chocolate ganache and a scoop of dreamy pistachio ice cream. Other desserts impress too — a fruit crisp, a good limey cheesecake, a chocolate cake with raspberry coulis — but none quite as much as the tarte.

The wine list is compelling, detailed, and includes wines by the half bottle, by the glass, and by the "flight."

BLACK CAT CAFÉ
93 Murray St. (between Parent and Dalhousie)
(613) 241-2999
www.blackcatcafe.ca
Access: One step up from street; washrooms are accessible
Price: Main dishes $18 to $28
Open: Lunch Mon.-Fri.; dinner Mon.-Sat.; closed Sun.

BLACK TOMATO

★★   Eclectic $$

The day the snow melts, the pretty courtyard patio is ready for business. I've seen parka people out there, warming hands over bowls of soup. Inside, the Black Tomato is a roomy, square space, high walls decked out with an eclectic collection of art. A handsome old-fashioned bar dominates one corner of the room. A couple of dozen glossy black tables set with floral mats are parked on the mature pine floors. Music is lively, quite terrific, and for sale in racks at the front door.

The Black Tomato menu sports a new look since my last visit, but its bill of fare remains unchanged, offering cuisine with a global reach.

There is a please-all list of starters — Thai-style soups, spanakopita, tostadas, curried chicken in phyllo, crab cakes, and an eclectic range of salads. From that list, the phyllo packages impress — tender chicken with grated vegetables and a pleasant sour hit of curry. The crab cakes do not; they're too raw-tasting, doughy, served with a red curry coconut sauce that's all frontal assault. A cold red pepper soup shines, bright with Asian flavours. A hot red pepper soup disappoints; short on roasted flavours and long on cream.

A baguette sandwich of succulent strips of grilled caribou and melted Brie makes a very satisfying lunch. At dinner, the tandoori lamb chops, charred to tender and wrapped with Indian spices, are the standout. Also good is the steak, pepper-crusted, garlic-rubbed, and served with caramelized red onions and wedges of herb-roasted potatoes. Tuna arrives two ways: as a thick square, grilled to rare, set in puddles of dill-infused oil; and in cold raw cubes "cooked" in a lime and dill anointment. Salmon is smoky-flavoured and moist, supported by a thick potato pancake, but strewn with vegetables that need a lot less crunch. The only real disappointments are a flabby vegetarian lasagna and later, a soggy cheesecake and a very lame raspberry crumble.

The Tomato servers are a young bunch, sometimes overextended, some of them under-trained (main dishes arrive before starters have been cleared), and some occasionally prefer to chat with each other than to deal with you. But if you're in no particular hurry, content to enjoy the music and the scene, then the payoff is that the Black Tomato food ranges from quite nice to quite delicious.

BLACK TOMATO
11 George St. (at Sussex)
(613) 789-8123
Access: Two steps at entrance; washrooms are on
main level but small
Price: Main dishes $15 to $25
Open: Daily for lunch and dinner

CAFÉ COMUS

★★ ½   **Canadian** $$$

When the Celtic Cross Pub moved out of this towering heritage space, Stratford-trained chef Jacqui Norris moved in. Together with her husband, who runs the front, Jacqui dishes up hearty bistro food in Almonte's old post office, about an hour's drive from Ottawa.

The tall walls are filled with big art and whimsical sculpture, all by local artists. There's still a pool table in the back room (a memento, I suppose, of its pub days), and despite the white linen and candles the space has its own quirky, homespun style. You may eat with some degree of anxiety over the possibility that your fine dining will be interrupted by the sound of kissing billiard balls. But worry not. Just accept that Comus hasn't quite figured out what it's all about yet, and enjoy Norris' compelling cooking.

The creamy-sharp goat cheese is local, as are most of the raw materials at Comus. It's supported by softly caramelized leeks and baked to bronze in butter-basted phyllo, served with organic field greens. The soup has vivid cauliflower flavour, patterned with a reduced balsamic glaze.

A risotto is flawless: the soup plate mounded with plump rice, coddled in mushroom stock to just the right degree of creamy-with-bite texture, the woodsy flavour potent, the whole overlaid with shards of sharp Parmesan. A fillet of salmon is moistened with a chive-studded mayonnaise and served with an aromatic pile of perfect wild rice.

Dessert is a totally delicious butter tart, plump with walnuts, perfumed with ginger, served with crème anglaise. The house crème brûlée, infused with local maple syrup, is very fine too.

Comus' wine list is all Canadian. The bottles are well chosen and kindly priced.

CAFÉ COMUS
73 Mill St. (at Little Bridge St.)
Almonte
(613) 256-6006
Access: Easy access into restaurant (small lip to negotiate);
washrooms are not wheelchair accessible
Price: Main dishes $16 to $25
Open: Lunch and dinner Tues.-Sat.

CAFÉ HENRY BURGER

★★★½ French $$$$

Over the eight-and-counting decades of its life—sometimes prosperous, sometimes troubled—Café Henry Burger has fed every prime minister in office, every newsmaker in Ottawa, and a good number of those who report on them, too. Its guest books are filled with a Who's Who of well-known names, and its handsome walls are lined with awards.

All things considered, you might be tempted to look for those telltale signs of a complacent business sitting on its laurels. You'll have to look elsewhere.

Robert Bourassa's Café Henry Burger doesn't serve dazzling, cutting edge cuisine—indeed, it rarely strays far from the French classics. But in this region, there is not another restaurant more concerned with excellence, or a kitchen more marked by old-fashioned expertise.

Just try the daily consommé. Duck is the basis of this well-flavoured, aromatic, oil-free broth. A tiny dice of vegetables—carrots, red pepper, zucchini—floats within the limpid, sparkling liquid. Likewise, the lobster bisque is a rich, perfumed soup of magnificent shellfish flavour, its velvety texture splashed with brandy and finished with cream.

They smoke their own salmon here. At lunch, three buttery slices of it are molded into rosettes, dotted with capers and set in a tangle of greens. At dinner, the same grand salmon is layered up with slices of soft potato, filled in with a sweet-and-tart confit of red onion. Thin rounds of fresh sea scallop marinated in lime juice are joined with an avocado mousse of fantastic flavour.

Main courses include a luscious veal chop, roasted pink, served "au jus" and surrounded, peasant-style, with lardons, sausage, perfect ovals of turned potato, and a sauté of wild and tame mushrooms. The fillet of salmon is meltingly good, perfectly undercooked, fragrant beneath a tomato-basil coulis. Finally, there's Alberta beef tenderloin, cooked rare as ordered, juicy, full of good beef flavour and scattered with chanterelle mushrooms.

A lunch fillet of salmon is glazed with maple syrup, roasted on a cedar plank, served with a buttery-sweet sauce pungent with mustard.

For dessert, there is much pleasure in the chocolate choices: the dark chocolate marquise with a pecan crust, set in crème anglaise and surrounded with fresh berries and dried pears; or the warm chocolate cake studded with pistachios. Also good is the house crêpe — very fresh, served with top-notch vanilla ice cream and a yummy apple caramel sauce.

Henry Burger's other assets include a staff that knows its business, a vast wine list, and a summer patio that overlooks the Museum of Civilization.

CAFÉ HENRY BURGER
69, rue Laurier (across from the Museum of Civilization)
Gatineau (Hull district)
(819) 777-5646
www.cafehenryburger.com
Access: Fully accessible
Price: Main dishes $28 to $39; table d'hôte $47
Open: Lunch Mon.-Fri.; dinner daily

CAFÉ PARADISO

★★   Eclectic $$$

We arrive on a Thursday night to a raucous, rocking restaurant, a room more suited to those with younger eardrums and less weary larynxes. The first room is wall-to-wall martini drinkers—a birthday party in the cocktail phase of its revelry. Later, the big group will move to its reserved tables for the sit-down phase of the evening and the music will switch from a steady bass beat to Diana Krall.

(Later still, a duo of jazz musicians will play delicious, moody music on the slightly raised section at the back of the room.)

Once you get beyond the cool, suave look of Paradiso, with its black leather benches, glass garage doors, melamine walls with oval-cut portholes, and retro-futuristic chandeliers right out of the *Jetsons*, you'll notice its other strengths. Like its servers: these handsome men know the food and the wine list, and they work very hard to please.

On the two-page menu you'll find lemongrass saté, steak-frites, soba noodles, and tandoori chicken pizza. Let's call it eclectic, or global, or whatever it is we call menus that defy neat categories. It charges in many directions, this food, sometimes with distinguished results, sometimes well off the mark.

Starters are hit and miss. Firmly in the "hits" are the calamari— impeccably grilled and tender squid, bathed in an Asian sauce potent with the anise flavour of Thai basil, presented on greens with pretty strings of beet and carrot. Also good are the crab cakes: texture fine, flavour fine, propped up with a zesty chipotle mayonnaise sweet with roasted garlic. We love the fresh salad of aromatic herbs with a starter of tuna—coriander, mint, and basil—but the rare slab of fish is thickly, overpoweringly crusted with sesame seeds. And the "salad rolls" are utterly flavourless. A construction of mango, peppers, vermicelli, and a tiny bit of basil wrapped in rice paper arrives stone cold, the noodles crunchy, the whole of it flavourless, and the sauce beside it tasting of thickened Fruitopia.

Back on track with the Paradiso salad: soft pear, sharp Asiago, and thin deep-fried lengths of prosciutto (lovely combination) over greens nutty with arugula in a ginger-potent dressing that's softened with orange and leek.

Two mains work, one doesn't. Lamb loins are crusted lightly (thank you) with pecans, cooked to medium-rare, and set in a wine reduction browned and rich with meaty flavour. The featured fish is mahi mahi, faultlessly cooked, sauced well. But the medium-rare bison is tough, quite unspectacular. Mascarpone-enriched mashed potatoes form the beds for these meats, this fish, but between the two is a layer of steamed carrot and zucchini desperate for seasoning.

At lunch, the steak-frites is good, fine, just not worth $23. A bowl of soba noodles and too-crunchy vegetables is treated with black bean sauce that doesn't quite reach the noodles, but rather puddles on the bottom. The seafood that crowns this largely flavourless mound is perfect, however.

Desserts are weak: the molten chocolate cake is dry, overbaked—missing the oozing of chocolate liquid at its centre, although the quality of the chocolate used is clearly fine. The blackcurrant cake tastes like something I'd get 30,000 feet up in the air.

It goes without saying the mixed drinks list is strong, but so too is the menu of wines with dozens of interesting (private stock) options by the glass and half-litre. There is a short insert of reserve wines.

CAFÉ PARADISO

199 Bank St. (between Nepean and Gloucester)
(613) 565-0657
www.cafeparadiso.ca
Access: Small lip into restaurant; washrooms are not wheelchair accessible
Price: Main dishes $16 to $25
Open: Lunch Mon.-Fri.; dinner daily

CAFÉ SHAFALI

★★★   Indian $

A warm fragrant breeze of Indian spices surrounds you as you enter this place. That's the first thing that strikes you about Café Shafali. Next, you notice the sumptuous art on the saffron-coloured walls, original oils by local artist Pieter Doef on sale for the benefit of Child Haven International. You wander around the art gallery before those spicy scents drive you back to your table and the Shafali menu.

And that's when you notice the wine suggestions that accompany many of Shafali's appetizers, curries, tandoori dishes and biryanis. You're told that a Merlot or a Beaujolais is the thing to have with the rogan josh, and that a semi-dry Riesling would pair best with the butter chicken.

While we examine the menu and wine suggestions, we order a round of Kingfisher beer (out of habit, I guess) and Shafali's appetizer platter.

You will do well to start this way, for the platter allows you a taste of Shafali's deep-fried packages—cumin-scented onion bhaji, cauliflower and spinach pakoras, spiced-up samosas, an oval of highly spiced ground beef strong of cinnamon and cardamom—plus some (sadly) dried-out chicken tikka from the tandoor.

The main dishes are divided into a collection of curries with headings like "bhoona" or "dhansak," followed by their respective descriptions: "cooked with tomato, pimento, onion, and spices, served in its own thick and rich gravy," or "a sweet-sour and fairly hot curry prepared in the Persian style with lentils." You pick the meat—chicken, lamb, beef, or shrimp. Some advice: begin mild. The butter chicken to start, perhaps, and then the lamb korma. Work your way up to the vindaloo.

A lamb pasanda is the colour of rich red mud and offers tender chunks of meat suffused with tandoori spices—particularly fragrant of cardamom and studded with apricots, raisins, and almonds. A mix of yellow and red lentils surrounds chunks of soft chicken in a hearty dhansak curry blended with ginger, garlic, fresh coriander, and the fragrant spices of garam masala—the whole considerably spiced up with the potent seeds of red and green chillies.

Fish is well treated: salmon is cooked with oranges, fresh coriander, and pungent ginger. Spinach, peppers, and onion coat crunchy shrimp in a sag curry. The naan is the only curious disappointment—too thick, too dry, missing that just-pulled-off-the-side-of-the-tandoor quality.

The service at this intimate café, provided by owner Gias Uddin, is personal and attentive.

CAFÉ SHAFALI

308 Dalhousie St. (between York and Clarence)
(613) 789-9188
www.shafali.com
Access: One step from street; washrooms are upstairs
Price: Main dishes $7.95 to $15.95
Open: Lunch Tues.-Sun.; dinner daily

CAM KONG

★★   Vietnamese $

We begin by inquiring about what beer is available, and receive only a puzzled look from our waitress. Another server, a young lad, informs us that Cam Kong is not licensed. Nor does it take credit cards or debit cards or cheques, as we discover at closing time. "Bank across street" is clearly a phrase our server has mastered.

So come with some cold hard cash in hand (you won't need much), and a thirst for nothing stronger than freshly-squeezed fruit juice and green tea.

But *do* come, for you will eat well here. Cam Kong's Vietnamese food is fresher and livelier than much I have eaten in this city.

There is joy and fun in this food—all that sizzling and stuffing and rolling and dipping and sharing that is Vietnamese cuisine, all that contrast of texture and flavour that can be varied, reworked, improved upon with each bite—more herbs, less noodle, more sprouts, less crunch, more crunch, more hot sauce, more mint.

It's all pretty more-ish at this place.

Start with the deep-fried wontons: the wrappers crisp and crumbly, the pork filling moist and well seasoned. Try too the spring rolls, those "French fries" of Asian cooking. Cam Kong's version stands out from the rest of the spring-roll crowd in this city for their flavour. (That is to say, they have some.)

We encountered not a single dud among the shrimp we sampled—sweet, crunchy, and encased in transparent rice paper with fresh basil and bean sprouts, packed vermicelli, and shreds of marinated carrot. You are given a fine peanut sauce in which to dunk them. This fresh shrimp roll best illustrates the glorious contrast of texture that is Vietnamese food.

Pho is Vietnamese beef noodle soup, and #202 arrives steaming and fragrant, the enormous basin of sweet, clear broth brimming with thin slices of tender rare beef, onion, and rice noodles. You can add bean sprouts, basil, lime juice, more nuoc nam, more hot sauce, if you wish.

Chicken is lightly battered and judiciously fried. On the side, you are served a cup of hot orange sauce tart with rind, thick with orange flavour. The Vietnamese quiche is a lovely wedge of egg custard, with strips of tender barbecue pork, more of those spring rolls, more lettuce, more bean sprouts, more dipping sauce . . . more good-looking, good-tasting fun on a platter.

CAM KONG

726 Somerset St. West (at Bell)
(613) 230-6815
Access: Four steps into restaurant from street level
Price: Main dishes $5.50 to $9.95
Open: Lunch and dinner every day except Tues.
No liquor licence
Cash only

CAPITAL ROOM

★★ ½   International $$$$

At first glance, the Delta Hotel dining room looks like it's been decorated by a naval taxidermist. A dozen glassed-in portholes protruding from its pale walls encase animals—fox, pheasant, mallards, and such. Other than these stuffed casements, it is a pleasant but viewless room—a trophy-case, men's-club sort of look.

You are greeted by the skilled maître d', made comfortable in plush armchairs at the considerately spaced tables, and served formally and well by the black-vested staff.

The daily menu is confined to two pages, and features straightforward hotel-ish dishes (beef tenderloin with a red wine sauce, veal porterhouse) mixed in with some more ambitious fare—sea scallops with a mushroom "crème brûlée," or tuna with a caramelized crust in a creamy lemongrass sauce.

A wild mushroom consommé is an amber broth, clean tasting, earthy and sweet, with long leaves of spinach and brown bundles of phyllo pastry bursting with peppery goat cheese. My only quibble is with the ungainliness of the spinach: some trimming would have been appreciated. The kitchen fashions thick brown crab cakes, well flavoured, set in a spicy red pepper sauce and served with a dill-flecked, sweetly roasted garlic aioli and a fresh and lively daikon salad.

The risotto is good, only somewhat overdone, the grains turned a pretty pink from being cooked in red wine, rich with chunks of gooey Gorgonzola cheese, perfumed with softly cooked onion and chopped dill, dotted with tiny cubes of red pepper and roasted corn. An appetizer of foie gras is paired with fresh figs and crisply fried rounds of leek and set in a dark reduced balsamic sauce. It is not, however, as seared as it should be, and there is some toughness to deal with.

As for the main dishes, results are mixed. The chicken breast (wing attached) is moist under its crust of mustard seed and rosemary, pleasantly served with a red onion and peach chutney. But the Brome Lake duck, which arrives medium-rare as requested, is disappointingly tough. While the sea scallops are clearly fresh and impeccably grilled, and the lobster sauce full-bodied, I find the wild mushroom "crème brûlée" with maple glaze a fascinating failure—too sweet, too fussy, too much. The rack of lamb is a generous serving of thick, pink chops, but the grill flavours are so pungent and the coarse salt coating so overpowering that the lamb flavour is lost. The tuna is very fresh and perfectly rare, but the poppyseed crust is annoying (crunch, crunch), and the so-called "spicy lemongrass cream Thai sauce" is bland and lemongrass-less.

Back to form with dessert, particularly with the house crème brûlée and a chocolate "decadence" cake, featuring layers of white chocolate mousse, dark chocolate mousse, and soft meringue.

The Capital Room offers a well-stocked wine list.

CAPITAL ROOM
Delta Ottawa Hotel, 361 Queen St. (at Lyon)
(613) 238-6000
www.deltahotels.com
Access: Fully wheelchair accessible
Price: Main dishes $24 to $38
Open: Lunch Mon.-Fri.; dinner Tues.-Sat.; closed Sun.

CARIBBEAN FLAVOURS

★ ★ ½   Caribbean $

If you're looking for a fast meal, walk on by. This little place, fairly new to the Somerset Street neighbourhood of mostly Asian eateries, offers à-la-minute Caribbean cooking. And that can mean many minutes' wait. Bring a few friends, sip your ginger beer, tap your Sorel boots to the warm reggae rhythms and—all in good time—your reward will be Caribbean cooking with heart, soul, and considerable fire.

The restaurant seats twenty-six at bare wooden tables, with room for three more at the bar. The walls are yellow above and pine-panelled below, interrupted by terracotta wainscoting. The requisite photo of Bob Marley shares space with some West Indian masks and sunny posters of island scenes. The joyous music helps to further the mood. What's missing from the picture is the crowd. Which is a pity.

Chef Frederick White's soups are homemade, rustic, light of texture, but deep of flavour. His cod cakes are fabulous—clearly just-assembled, substantial but delicate too, served with a thyme- and chilli-flecked sauce of considerable oomph. A shrimp starter is a plate of ho-hum small shrimp, tough and tasteless, but livened considerably by their very spicy creole sauce.

And then there are the jerk wings, which have major wow. Jerk marinades, dry rather than wet, of allspice, thyme, bay leaves, peppercorns, and considerable quantities of hot peppers, are not to be sneezed at. These wings, ordered "medium," arrive blisteringly hot. If you like that, you'll like these. We needed bowls of yogurt to manage the next round.

A gentle beef curry is a dark, heavy dish of very tender meat in a very rich sauce with very little bite. With the stew comes much else — rice and peas, braised carrots, steamed green beans, chayote, butternut squash, okra, grilled sweet potato, and plantain, each one perfectly done. Codfish and ackee, a national dish of Jamaica, is superb here, cooked with onions, tomato, and lots of black pepper and spices. Goat curry is a moist, tender stew with a medium curry bite, served with a homemade mango chutney of gloriously ripe mango flavour. Starchy, faintly sweet grilled plantain is curled next to thick strips of very moist, very tender chicken, marked with the black stripes and fragrance of the grill, and treated to a sharp sauce based on Chef White's homemade ginger beer.

The rôti at Caribbean Flavours are just-fried-up-fresh and can cradle a variety of tender, well-flavoured curries — chicken, beef, goat, codfish, potato, vegetable, channa, or tofu.

For dessert, a banana flambé, with crème anglaise, a puddle of homemade strawberry sauce, and Jamaican Bounty rum. The assembly is lit at the table until the sauce and the banana begin to caramelize, then the fire is blown out before all the rum leaves. Fabulous.

CARIBBEAN FLAVOURS

881 Somerset St. West (at Preston)
(613) 237-9981
www.caribbeanflavours.net
Access: Steps into restaurant; washrooms are small
Price: Rôtis and main dishes $6.50 to $16.95
Open: Lunch and dinner Tues.-Sun.; closed Mon.

CASTLEGARTH

★★★   **Canadian – Eclectic**   **$$**

It's about a fifty-minute drive from downtown Ottawa, west to Arnprior, then south on Highway 2 to White Lake Village. When you get there, go west on the Burnstown Road. Castlegarth restaurant is on the right. If the sign still hasn't made it up (they were rather busy with wedding preps when I visited) just roll down the windows: you should be able to sniff it out.

This is the old Stirling House, a heritage building dating back to the mid-1800s. It's now owned by a couple of twentysomething kids: Jennifer Ross and Matthew Brierly, graduates of the Stratford Chefs School. Our fall dinner at Castlegarth took place a week before their wedding.

The Brierly-Ross menu is a one-page deal, and it changes daily. No dish requires more than a few words by way of explanation. The style is pure, clean, and ingredient-driven; organic, fresh, and based on the pleasures of the seasons.

In early September, the pleasures are many and obvious, bursting out of the earth. Homage to what is seasonal in the unforgiving climate of the Ottawa Valley is a challenge. Plans are in the works, we're told, to build greenhouses to grow produce year-round. Perhaps I'll return in February and have another taste. My first was pure pleasure.

To start: vibrant Bryson Farms greens surround magnificent sea scallops, paired with crunchy-fried straw potatoes. An abundance of heirloom tomatoes feature in a simple ricotta- and basil-enhanced tomato salad. I have never tasted better. Roasted garlic, more of those magnificent tomatoes, and roughly chopped basil join olives, anchovies, and capers in an intensely flavoured shallow bowl of linguine puttanesca.

Pork tenderloin, all its good pork flavour intact, is paired with a late-summer peach chutney. The surface of a fillet of fresh rainbow trout is salted and crunchy, its inside buttery and moist. It's served with fluffy, nubbly couscous, early autumn vegetables, and a roasted red pepper stuffed with roasted tomatoes. The steak is an assertively flavoured piece of meat, cooked well, surrounded with new potatoes and summer vegetables. Rustic chunks of medium-rare lamb are set in a light jus, sweet with roasted garlic, surrounded with red chard, chickpeas, and tomatoes.

The vanilla bean–infused crème brûlée is everything a classic should be.

Given the quality of the product, Castlegarth's prices are considerably lower than you'd find in Ottawa. The wine list, like the menu, is short, but includes some interesting finds and is remarkable too for its kind prices.

The other great pleasure of the place is Jennifer Ross herself, who attends to our table with obvious skill and unaffected charm.

CASTLEGARTH
90 Burnstown Rd. (at White Lake Rd.)
White Lake Village
(613) 623-3472
Access: One step to negotiate
Price: Main dishes $15 to $22
Open: Dinner only, Wed.-Sun.

CEYLONTA

★★   Sri Lankan – South Indian $

We arrive shortly after one o'clock to find a queue at the front door. Other people appear from the direction of the dining room and form behind us. It takes a few minutes to register that this is a procession for the cash register: diners clutching ten-dollar bills to cover the $8.95 cost of the daily lunch buffet. A woman leaves the line and returns with one more hastily snatched urid dahl "donut" from the buffet table around the corner.

"They're pretty addictive," she says, smiling sheepishly.

Ceylonta's owner, Ranjan Thana, apologizes for the wait and suggests that the buffet looked better at 11:30. He's probably right. The tablecloth is splattered, the string hoppers are congealed, the naan is rock hard. In the time it takes us to order a mango lassi and a Kingfisher beer, though, things have been tidied and the buffet replenished.

Here and there in these plain rooms and on the Ceylonta menu, there is information about Sri Lankan food. A photo is framed in Ceylon spices — coriander, cumin, fenugreek, cardamom, curry leaves, fennel seed, cinnamon bark, black mustard seed. We look, we read, and then we head to the food to further our education.

Fresh string hoppers have just arrived. So has a basket of just-fried urid dahl cakes. We load up on these addictive donuts and the accompanying coconut sambal, along with the chewy, spicy, fried sprates (sardines). There is a plain, lightly perfumed salad of red onion and tomato onto which we dollop some yogurt. Then basmati rice and the various curries. There is a "black" curry of lentils and another one of chickpeas, splendid with cardamom and fennel, the dark colour achieved by the Sri Lankan technique of fast-roasting herbs and spices to dark brown before grinding them. And then a "red" curry of beef and potatoes (lots of chillies, fewer spices). For a usually meek, please-all buffet—as buffets tend to be—these dishes approach authentic in the scorching department. The milder curries—one of whole-leaf spinach and one of curried squash—are splendid with onion, fennel seed, and cardamom pods, and sweet with grated coconut.

Accompanying the curries are spicy condiment: marinated dried red chillies, the mild and nubbly coconut sauce, a cooling yogurt, and sprates: deep-fried, crunchy, their flavour heightened with chilli, onion, salt, and lime.

If you stick with the dark meat and avoid the breast, the tandoori chicken is moist, falling-off-the-bone tender, and dripping with its reddened marinade.

À la carte, you can order the dosai: platter-sized south Indian crêpes, wrapped around a filling of curried goat. There is sambar (a spicy lentil and vegetable soup), which you can ladle on top if you wish. For dessert, there is tapioca pudding, sweet with coconut milk, and there are the gulab jamun dumplings, very moist, infused with the sweet, aromatic syrup that surrounds them.

Ceylonta isn't much from the curb. But inside, there is the warmth of gracious service, the grand flavours of good food, and a bill that is remarkably fair.

CEYLONTA
403 Somerset St. West (between Kent and Bank)
(613) 237-7812
www.ceylonta.com
Access: Fully accessible
Price: Main dishes $6.95 to $11.95; lunch buffet $8.95
Open: Daily for lunch and dinner

CLAIR DE LUNE

★★★   French – Contemporary $$$

It's a bittersweet time of year when the last basket of peaches leaves the market stalls and the first load of pumpkins arrives. Our first visit to Clair de Lune was on a balmy late-September evening, and the chilled peach soup seemed absolutely perfect. A mere two weeks later, in the driving sleet, we're met with a thick purée of roasted root vegetables, sweet with caramelized parsnip, salty with crisp bacon — just exactly what we want.

Welcome to Ottawa: twenty-two above on Monday, two below on Thursday.

We are weather people. We eat to celebrate it, and we eat to find comfort from it. Clair de Lune responds. Its monthly menu is boosted by daily specials that show that someone in its kitchen has stepped outside and figured out it's a hot-pumpkin-soup kind of day, and that the chilled peach had better be gone.

Clair de Lune has also responded to the drive to redecorate: its twenty-year-old entrance is now lime green. Other walls are blue and burgundy. Large oil canvasses are vibrant with more colour. For a mid-week lunch, we are seated on a long scarlet bench on the first of three levels. Two gilded mirrors hang on the brick wall above us. The lights affixed to the pressed tin ceiling form a geometric maze of colour: blue, red, white, and yellow squares. The bar is long, inlaid with glass block and filled with regulars. Clair de Lune's owner for all those years, Adel Ayad, greets them all.

The wee pumpkins on the tables are a pleasing seasonal touch. We only wish there was candlelight too, and that the Rubik's cube of multi-lights above us could be dimmed. The room feels too bright for dinner.

An amuse-bouche arrives as we examine the one-page menu: a moist chunk of salmon on a slice of cucumber. It's fine, nothing more.

Nothing dull about the Caesar, though: its pungent, lemon-zinged dressing coats the fresh hand-torn leaves of romaine. It's way better than the mixed salads we are given at lunch; some leaves are limp, others marked, and the mix seems to have been prepared a while ago. The dressing, however, is sprightly: a fruity vinaigrette pungent with Dijon.

Seedy mustard and capers are the zing in a starter of salmon rillettes, featuring the fresh and smoked fish together in a moist, fibrous, and flavourful fusion. Mussels are brilliant, steamed in a sauce laced with Indonesian flavours. A smoky terrine of red pepper and eggplant is boosted with a well-garlicked tomato sauce, served with a goat-cheese crostini.

The skin could be crispier, but the meat is fall-off-the-bone tender in the confit of lamb. Its side of garlic-rubbed Yukon golds, sliced and baked to golden brown in oil and butter, is fabulous, as are the caramelized parsnips that flank it. Our other mains are all from the sea, a strong section of this menu. Five fat, snappy shrimp are impeccably fresh, perfectly grilled, and bathed in a ginger-soy-citrus dressing. They're supported by a cold spinach salad, though, rather than the wilted greens and grilled root vegetables we were promised.

The cheesecake is pumpkin, smooth and rich, troubled only by an over-exuberance of nutmeg. The profiteroles are bathed in a glorious chocolate sauce, filled with splendid ice cream, the choux puffs tasting just-baked. Clair de Lune's crème caramel is smooth and cool, with candied orange rind in the Grand Marnier caramel.

The wine list is considerably longer than the menu. In addition to the regular list, there is an insert. "Les sélections du sommelier" are limited-quantity wines, in a price range that starts at $24 and climbs to $250. There are half-bottles on this list. Champagne by the glass, too. How refreshing is that?

CLAIR DE LUNE

81B Clarence St. (between Dalhousie and Parent)
(613) 241-2200
www.clairdelune.ca
Access: One small lip up from street level; main dining room is accessible (two other rooms are up a few steps); washrooms are downstairs
Price: Main dishes $17 to $32
Open: Daily for lunch and dinner

CYRANOS

★★ ½   **Mediterranean** $$

Here's a Robertson Road strip-mall restaurant that manages to banish the mall atmosphere from the dining room. It's been cast out by clever lighting, bold paint, and the arresting canvasses of fruits and vegetables plastered along the west wall. The focal point of the place is the big, open kitchen at the back, rather than the largely automotive view out the front windows. Candles, fresh flowers, soft lighting, an impressive bar, and voila! Robertson Road has stepped out of the picture.

Which is a good thing.

Good things come from this kitchen, too.

The menu offers predictable starters like calamari, Caesar salad, and mussels. These are followed by a selection of pizzas, a page of fresh pasta, and main dishes that feature various ways with veal, chicken, steak, and fish. You've seen it before. But here, it works.

There is no shyness of flavour in the deep-fried, feta-stuffed phyllo pastries served with a mint-fresh, garlic-potent yogurt sauce. A starter of grilled vegetables offers smoky, charred eggplant and sweet peppers with creamy-sharp goat cheese smoothing the edges, the construct anointed with good balsamic. A carrot-dill soup has its heart in the right place, but needs two pinches more salt to punch up the flavour.

The pastas at Cyranos shine. Made in-house and properly cooked, the linguine comes with streaks of prosciutto and loads of fresh mushrooms, perfumed with thyme and rich with flavour. The tomato sauce that clings to the penne has big tomato flavour, and the sausages do their job of spicing up the dish.

More eggplant, charred in all the right places, combined with sun-dried tomatoes and goat cheese, features on a pizza crust that's chewy and sweet.

Halibut is perfectly baked with a brick-red pepper sauce perked up with capers.

Cyranos' desserts are noteworthy, and the house lemon pudding takes the cake.

CYRANOS
39 Robertson Rd. (Bell Mews Plaza)
(613) 721-0510
Access: Fully accessible
Price: Main dishes $13 to $24
Open: Lunch Mon.-Fri.; dinner Mon.-Sat.; closed Sun.

DALY'S

★★   French – Contemporary $$$$

The long-awaited rejuvenation of the dining room of the Westin Hotel was completed in March 2002. The new Daly's is on the same long, curved, third-floor landscape. It boasts the same pleasing view and can accommodate the same number of diners. But that's about where the sameness ends. The new look is understated elegance. The colours are inviting, the lighting is warm and flattering, and the furnishings, accessories, tableware, and stemware are of a more pampered class. It is a hotel dining room with an unfussy, well-appointed feel.

A late spring dinner at Daly's was impressive. A follow-up lunch was roundly disappointing. Clearly, the challenges of the 24/7 hotel kitchen remain.

Dinner began with a celery root soup of terrific flavour, followed by crispy red tuna rolls, which were very fresh and quite wonderful. And then sweetbreads, perfectly cooked, sweetened with apples, piqued with cider vinegar, served with greens and roasted shallots. The last starter was scallops, cooked with an exquisitely light touch, served with a tatsoi and lemongrass sauce.

Of the main dishes, the signature "tuile" of lamb was showmanship that worked: perfectly rare, gloriously tender chops jutting out from tall, savoury, crinkly wafers, with roasted vegetables and fava beans for company. An earthy dish of roasted guinea hen came layered with fragrant cabbage and lardons, the tender meat sweetened with wedges of soft green apple. Finally, a wholly more sophisticated dish of supple lobster, rich flavour intact, in a heady sauce liberally doused with cognac and garnished with a well-done risotto spiked with overdone mushrooms.

Lunch was less encouraging. Despite its state-of-the-art heated tables (rather than chafing dishes) and food stylishly displayed in crockery (rather than steel), the usual buffet bricks of petrified quiche and shrunken food remain. A cream of asparagus soup was inedibly salty, clam fritters were soggy, crab cakes were doughy and tasted strong of iodine, veal was tough, chicken Parmesan was rubbery, beef and asparagus rolls were just plain dried out. The pretty salad bar was a display of over-chilled and flavourless offer-ings — an Asian noodle salad of no Asian flavour, a cold, astringent tabbouleh, a potato salad of waterlogged potatoes, California rolls of cold, tired rice — and so on. Eliminating three quarters of the food and concentrating on the quality of what's left would help here.

Two desserts I'd order again: a magnificent lemon tart, and a rich but not overly sweet mascarpone mousse cake.

DALY'S
Westin Hotel
11 Colonel By Dr. (at Daly)
(613) 560-7333
www.westinottawa.com
Access: Fully accessible
Price: Main dishes $21 to $34
Open: Daily for breakfast, lunch, and dinner

DOMUS CAFÉ

★★★★   Canadian $$$$

You may look, but you will never find an asparagus soup on John Taylor's January menu. In early June, it's a different matter. Then the fleshy young shoots will feature prominently, comme il faut.

Taylor's cooking is driven by impeccable raw materials from farms and foragers that meet his standards and values. His monthly menu gives credit to those providers, and presents their wares in ways that express the food's aesthetic pleasure and the time of the year in which it shines. His menus are Taylor-made to show off a season's bounty. His food shows he's at the top of his game. The sleek, unfussed-over look of his café shows that it's the food that matters here.

On a January menu, a starter of foie gras (from Mariposa Farms) arrives flash-grilled, its surface darkly bronzed, its inside meltingly soft, its flavour deeply satisfying. It rests on slices of grilled brioche. Beside it is a wee runny quail egg, sunny side up, a scattering of caramelized pearl onion, and a spoon of grated apple, crimson in a cider reduction, sweet, tart and magnificent with the liver. For the "full foie," accept a glass of Stoney Ridge ice wine.

Mushroom risotto is splendid here—made with all the care, thought, and attention to complementary tastes and textures that the dish demands. We are fed faultless steak-frites: quality meat, properly aged, grilled right, served with grilled portobellini mushrooms, a sticky reduction of beef and mushroom jus, a mound of big, fat fries, and a homemade mayonnaise livened with horseradish. When you're in the mood, it doesn't get much better.

Skate is the fish selection, soft and buttery, if a little too intensely salted. It comes with whole scallions fried in a tempura batter, red jacket potatoes, and spinach. Ontario quail, bronzed and succulent, rests on Asian flavours: a miso-and-sesame-treated broth with greens, rice noodles, and shiitake mushrooms.

A Domus lunch looks like this: an intensely flavoured wild and tame mushroom soup with goat cheese and a swirl of green canola oil, and then a great pile of nutty arugula dotted with toasted hazelnuts, goat feta, and balsamic-sweetened red onions, dressed with a mustard vinaigrette. Thin slices of Parmesan and fried foccaccia croutons crown a long braise of white beans, interrupted by roasted root vegetables, chunks of beef shank, and some good smoky bacon.

Favourite Domus desserts include a textbook crème brûlée and a warm "stew" of wintery fruits atop a moist spice cake filled with crème fraîche.

As you'd expect, given Taylor's regional values, the bulk of Domus' extensive wine list is Canadian bottles, with lots of interesting choices by the glass or half-litre.

DOMUS CAFÉ
85 Murray St. (at Dalhousie)
(613) 241-6007
www.domuscafe.ca
Access: Fully accessible
Price: Main dishes $22 to $40
Open: Brunch/lunch daily; dinner Mon.-Sat.

DON ALFONSO

★★   Spanish $$

There's not an ounce of pretension. No high-end interior design concepts, either: the walls are wide, dark planks, tin lanterns dangle from the barn beams, and a big barrel bottom is mounted on the wall. Coats are on display on the pipe rack, booster chairs above, chafing dishes on the buffet table beside. On every thick wooden table, set with thick wooden chairs, sits an oil lamp.

The more you know this place, the better you like it. You'll be drawn to the exuberant, kindly service; and as you become familiar with the strengths of this kitchen, you'll steer to the good food.

For something like twenty-three years, Alfonso Garcia of Galicia, Spain, has been dishing up the tapas. Some of them are quite wonderful: a simple preparation of quartered field mushrooms, fried up in garlic, garlic, and (did I mention?) garlic served in a winy, oily, parsley-thick broth. Lots of hot crunchy shrimp arrive in a bubbling sauce rich with oil and (yes) garlic, every drop of which we mop up with excellent Portuguese buns.

Not everything is perfect. The house squid is tender and fresh, but fried up in oil that isn't. The day's soup is a very average cream of vegetable, its flavour strong of cream and weak of vegetable. And I know gazpacho is standard on every Spanish restaurant of this ilk, and if I were in Galicia, I'd likely order it—but in Ottawa in November, it ain't happening. Best wait for August.

We enjoy the seafood paella, although it suffers—like every "authentic" paella I have ever had—from overcooked seafood. It is nevertheless a good-looking dish, with a bed of saffron-scented, seafood-soaked rice dotted with sweet peas and red peppers. And the seafood, despite having been buried in all that hot rice too long, is still flavourful and plentiful.

Outside of the paella, the fish fares better. There are a generous quantity of perfectly soft-fleshed, deeply caramelized scallops set in a creamy sauce, green with parsley, served with pea-studded rice. And you will do well to order the fresh halibut special for its fine Provençale sauce, briny with olives.

For dessert, the flan, with its lovely bittersweet caramel, is a better option than the chocolate mousse cake, which is clearly not made in-house. The medicinal aftertaste of edible oil products clings to it.

There's a fine selection of Iberian wines on this list. When we ask about one, our sweet server hasn't a clue, and says so. "I'll bring you a glass," she says, "and if you don't like it, I'll bring you a different one." We like it. We like her. Indeed, what's not to like?

DON ALFONSO
434 Bank St. (at Gladstone)
(613) 236-7750
www.donalfonso.ca
Access: Stairs at entrance; washrooms are downstairs
Price: Main dishes $12.95 to $27; table d'hôte $22.95
Open: Lunch Mon.-Fri.; dinner Mon.-Sun.

EAST INDIA COMPANY RESTAURANT

★★ ½   Indian $$

A well-established family-run restaurant from Winnipeg brought a 400-year-old south Indian bridal carriage to Ottawa. It was to be the focal point of the family's second restaurant. When it wouldn't fit through the front doors, so the story goes, the windows were taken out. And now it rests, along with some slighter but no less impressive antiques, in the front foyer of this 2002 addition to the Indian restaurant scene in Ottawa.

The East India Company is a vast restaurant with a definite "wow" factor. Along with the carriage, there are roaring lions at the entrance, century-old tablets from an Indian temple, pieces of sandstone walls, and elaborate hand-stitched hangings. The walls are the colour of the tandoori chicken.

On the evening buffet you will find substance to match this style. The chicken is melt-in-the-mouth, the flesh smoky and moist, the reddened surface scorched in the intense heat of the tandoor. The shrimp are fresh and crunchy in a clever harmony of onion, tomatoes, and garam masala spices, smoothed with coconut milk. They're also good buried within a mound of basmati rice (which is too assertively fragrant of clove for my liking). We met two fine meat choices on the buffet: Ontario lamb, on the bone, cooked in a tomato-based curry of no heat but wonderful depth, and a whole Cornish hen, immensely flavourful, juicy, and searingly hot.

A variety of vegetarian curries are on offer: roasted eggplant, mashed with soft onions, tomatoes, garlic, ginger, spices; and navratan, a sweet, mild mixed-vegetable dish dotted with fresh Indian cream cheese. Channa masala means chickpeas: less sweet, less rich, and a whole lot less mild.

You may also order à la carte. Deep-fried starters are all remarkably ungreasy, served with a coriander-mint chutney and also a sweet and sour brown sauce based on tamarind.

Discs of flattened dough are slung onto the scorching sides of the cavernous tandoori oven. This naan is as fresh as it gets. There are flavoured ones if you want—garlic naan, cheese, vegetable, herbed. A bit much, perhaps, but all good.

There seems no shortage of staff to wait on tables, monitor the buffet, whisk away dirty plates, or package up uneaten curries into bags for the trip home.

EAST INDIA COMPANY RESTAURANT
210 Somerset St. West (between Elgin and Metcalfe)
(613) 567-4634
Access: Fully accessible
Price: Main dishes $11.95 to $18.95; dinner buffet $16.95
Open: Lunch Sun.-Fri.; dinner daily

EIGHTEEN

★★★   **French – Contemporary** $$$$

Note: As this book goes to press, Eighteen has acquired a new Executive Chef. Neil Mather is currently working with John Leung's menu, but is expected to launch his own sometime in the spring of 2004.

When Eighteen first opened in 2001, my expectations were high. This was not, after all, the standard Irish pub makeover of a derelict Byward Market building. This was a thoroughly urban eatery, stunning and sleek, wrapped in the thick limestone walls that reminded us we were still in Ottawa.

But in its early days I rarely ate a meal, or experienced service, as pleasurable as the setting. Mostly, I felt this newcomer was little more than a high-end, low-lit bar for the well-heeled martini drinker.

Much of my concern vanished when Chef John Leung was brought on board. His short menu of contemporary French food with exotic touches offers some of the best reading in town.

Foie gras to start, served with a nutty polenta and a dark sauce spiked with brandy and maple syrup. Then seared tuna loin, vibrating with freshness, perfectly rare, served with a warm salad of shiitake mushrooms livened with citrus leaf and splashed with a mango vinaigrette. Squid is grilled and fabulously tender, fragrant of lemongrass and Thai basil, served on a mound of grated zucchini and sweetened with milky garlic. A final starter course of duck, seared to medium-rare and laced with five-spice powder, rests on sliver-thin slices of orange beets, corn shoots, and a tangle of deep-fried taro root. Fantastic.

The main courses are just as entertaining: pork loin, rubbed hard with hot spices ("eighteen" of them, we're told) and then roasted to bronze, served as three thick succulent slabs. A mélange of sweet potato, wilted frisée, and chunks of Gorgonzola accompany the pork. Mahi mahi is slightly over-exuberantly salted, but rescued by a broth (fish stock, lime juice, and coriander) that isn't. The fish is supported with a light risotto, not particularly creamy or rich, but of the proper risotto consistency, greened with peas and coriander. A chicken breast is extraordinary for its simple goodness—full of juicy flavour, its skin treated lightly with sea salt, beautifully browned. The chicken is escorted by a fabulous wedge of potato and sweet little haricots verts strewn with caramelized onions.

Pepper mills are a feature on every table. (We like that.) Wine suggestions are given with every dish. (We like that, too.) Eighteen's wine list is a leather-bound short story that begins with a philosophy of wine (they like the stuff), then moves on through a page of featured wines, a list of "flights," two dozen wines available by the glass, more by the half-bottle (including champagne—we *really* like that), a page of French wines divided by region, and then four more pages of largely New-World wines. Dessert and ice wines follow (mostly Canadian), and then the list of Left Bank premier cru.

Then: "Forgive me for interrupting, but shall I bring our dessert menu?" How to refuse such civility?

The double chocolate tart with mascarpone cheese is thrilling, as is its ginger brandy-snap accessory. And the lemon mousse terrine is fine. Less thrilling are the crispy banana cigars, fried in wontons and a bit stodgy for my liking—although who'd have thought green tea and lemon thyme would be so brilliant together in a ball of ice cream?

EIGHTEEN
18 York St. (at Sussex)
(613) 244-1188
www.restaurant18.com
Access: With notice given, a ramp is available to access the dining room; washrooms are not accessible.
Price: Main dishes $25 to $34
Open: Lunch Mon.-Fri.; dinner Mon.-Sat.; closed Sun

EL MESON

| ★★★   Spanish – Portuguese $$ |

Owner Jose Alves stocks over a hundred wines in this gracious New Edinburgh restaurant. Many are Portuguese reds, about which I have no clue. No worries, though: he's available to chat about them. He likes doing that. Much like garlic in this cuisine, Mr. Alves is everywhere. He's a large part of the appeal of this well-regarded Iberian restaurant.

Order one of his Portuguese wine suggestions and just see how well it handles the sopa de ajo — a stout broth pungently infused with garlic, and fortified with chopped chorizo sausage and lightly cooked egg.

El Meson's shrimp à la ajillo features more of that omnipresent bulb, the shrimp crunchy in an oily, winy broth, green with parsley, touched with cream. A plate of calamares is tender and toothsome; a basin of clams is fired up in a vinegar-splashed broth with tomatoes, bay leaves, thyme, garlic, and potent Brazilian peppers.

Main dishes continue the concentration on seafood. There is good paella here, the shrimp, scallops, mussels fresh and only slightly overcooked, the fish perfectly yielding. There's sausage too, of course, biting and fatty, and chicken that's tender enough, all buried in moist, sweet-spiced, fragrant rice.

The zarzuela is an ample casserole in which the seafood is plunged into a well-flavoured, garlicky broth, steaming hot, scented with herbs and splashed with cognac. Hunks of firm, succulent salmon are smothered with onions, olives, garlic, and oil, served with roast potatoes, roast beets, green beans, cauliflower, and broccoli, all impeccable.

But it's not all about fish—the beef can hold its own too. The solomillos Portuguesa is a perfectly rare fillet, fragrant with cepes, garlic, chorizo sausage, and peppers.

An iceberg of poached meringue protrudes from a vanilla custard, drizzled with caramel. We like this best. Good too is the classic crema catalana and an almond cake, dense, nutty, not too sweet and very fresh.

EL MESON
94 Beechwood Ave. (at Springfield)
(613) 744-8484
www.elmeson.ca
Access: Steps into restaurant; washrooms are downstairs
Price: Main dishes $14 to $26
Open: Lunch Mon.-Fri.; dinner daily

EMPIRE GRILL

★★ ½   **New American** $$$

"Guaranteed to go down quickly." That is *not* my comment on this Byward Market restaurant. It was the description of a martini called the "Bre-X" on the Empire Grill drinks list when it first opened in 1998. The Bre-X martini is no longer around. Today, the cocktails have American titles: the Bronx Bachelor, the Yankee Thriller, Harlem Nights. For Canadian titles, you now have to turn to the well-constructed, food-matching-friendly wine list of about eighty names, where the Canadian content is high. (Agreeably large, too, is the number of wines available by the glass and half-bottle.)

Drinks are a large part of what the Empire Grill is about. So are the scene and the style. There is an energy here that settles in every corner, but the room has been designed in such a way that privacy, even intimacy, can be found if that's what you want. The atmosphere has much to do with its wonderful curves, soft lighting, and use of dark wood screens to craft separate spaces.

So, it has great booze and visual drama—what about the food?

From back in 1998, I remember a largely Mediterranean menu of pretty tedious stuff. There are still pizzas, and a few pasta creations, but Chef Mohamed Yusuf's menu is now much more about top-notch ingredients on the grill—meat and fish—dressed with global flair. It's a menu that allows you to go all out with foie gras and a porterhouse steak, or go easy with mussels and fries.

Whatever you do, start with the seafood chowder. Smoked mackerel in the mix of mussels, crab, shrimp, and firm root vegetables, lends a magnificent smoky flavour to the rich broth. For $7, it's one of the better chowders of my life. Smoky too are the sea scallops, grilled to rare inside, their brush with truffle oil likely responsible for their exquisite flavour. Three of them lie atop a mound of risotto, potent with parmigiano flavour, the construct littered with deep-fried sticks of leek and edible flower petals. Ordinarily, fish and cheese are no match, but these scallops can take on this rice, and both come out on top.

Good heavens, more fish — and the disappointment of the evening. Priced at $29, it's a bitter one. The seafood platter in the "Sharing Plates" section of the menu is a disaster: mealy, overcooked mussels, desiccated salmon, rock-hard scallops, a lobster and vermicelli rice-paper roll of no flavour whatsoever, and two I-don't-know-what-to-do-with-them crayfish (where's the fork?). There's some relief, mind you, in three one-bite crab cakes, which are moist and tasty with their wee dollop of chipotle mayo, and the hoisin-treated shrimp are terrific. It's a lot to pay for those few bites, though.

On to better things. The veal chop is thick and meaty, expertly grilled to medium rare, with a saltimbocca smack of fresh sage and prosciutto. Soft portobello mushrooms sing balsamic flavours in a perfect wine and lamb jus reduction. It is very good. The sauce is the thing too with the chicken fettuccini, its flavour heightened by the juice of roasted vegetables. Garlic, red peppers, and shallots are part of the sauce, but so are sun-dried tomatoes, marinated artichokes, portobello mushrooms, spinach, and basil. Oh yes, and chicken. Soft enough, but not the highlight of this dish.

A medicinal-tasting crème caramel and passable profiteroles (good chocolate sauce, though) are garnished with sickly-sweet whipped cream. Service throughout is wonderful, though — nothing's too much trouble for our big handsome man.

EMPIRE GRILL

47 Clarence St. (at Parent)

(613) 241-1343

www.empiregrill.com

Access: Easy access into restaurant; regular washrooms are downstairs, but there's a fully accessible washroom in the neighbouring mall

Price: Main dishes $12 to $33

Open: Daily for lunch, dinner, and late dining

FAIROUZ

★ ★ ½   Lebanese $$

Lebanese is a cuisine we encounter most often on Styrofoam plates in cacophonous food courts. But Fairouz offers opulence, with china and all the right forks, in a lovely old house in the Somerset Village strip. And Fairouz has maintained the standards that have made it Ottawa's go-to restaurant for fine Lebanese dining.

It cooks the way it always has, with many of the traditional dishes offered on a menu that's strictly à la carte. (There is a typed insert of "specials," but these seem to be just dishes plucked from the regular menu and highlighted.)

A plate of mezze contains most of what you want to start things off. Two are warm: super-fresh sambosik — phyllo-wrapped feta with spinach, baked brown; and flavour-packed cylinders of ground lamb and bulghur, delicately scented with cinnamon, allspice and pepper. The balance of the plate is cool: tabbouleh with abundant parsley, tartly flavoured with lemon; and a fattoush salad, freshly assembled, aromatic, its trademark pita "croutons" clearly just-fried. And then two dollops of dip: a smooth, brightly seasoned hummus bi tahini and a glorious, pungent baba ghanoush, the purée of cooked eggplant smoky-tasting from the charring of its purple skin.

Main dishes include pink lamb loins of good lamb flavour, covered with sharp grainy Dijon and tempered with cream. There are chicken livers, tender in their oil, lemon, and sweet pomegranate soak. There is fresh salmon, wrapped in coriander and lemon, swimming in garlic-soused juices.

The one disappointment is the quail, which is tender and forceful in its char-grilled flavour, but has a stewy texture.

Sweets are authentically so. Atayef is a crêpe filled with a rich, thick sweet custard, sprinkled with pistachios and scented with rose-water. If that's not your cup of tea, go straight to the stout coffee.

There is a selection of Lebanese wines to go with this food, and Fairouz' owner is only too pleased to show them off.

FAIROUZ
343 Somerset St. West (at Metcalfe)
(613) 233-1536
www.fairouz.ca
Access: Steps up to restaurant; washrooms are downstairs; sidewalk patio is accessible
Price: Main dishes $15 to $19
Open: Lunch Mon.-Fri.; dinner daily

FIORI

★★   Italian $$$

It seems to me they've removed *some* of the photos of former owner Pasquale DiCintio from the foyer of Fiori, but not all. My understanding is that the new owners, the Tatsis family, are friends of DiCintio, which likely explains why he's still hanging out on the restaurant's walls.

I returned to Fiori after a three-year absence to see what was new. The answer was "not much." Same décor, same two formal rooms, even (seemed to me) the same tiny gentleman I remember from a few years ago to serve (correctly and quietly) our choice table by the front window.

But the menu looks different — God's on the cover now — and inside is a new lineup of dishes, many sporting "house specialty" asterisks. Mostly, though, these are the same northern Italian dishes we see everywhere else.

What is new and laudable is the "lista del vino," which stands out for its thoughtful and helpful directions. The list is divided into Italy's wine regions, complete with map, and provides a description of each one and a few affordable choices beneath each explanation. It then offers a dozen or so wines from other wine regions, including a 2002 Niagara Ratafia, described as a "dangerously delicious sipper." (Priced at $92 for a half-bottle, it would be dangerous if it weren't.) Back to Italy for two packed pages of mostly big reds — some available by the glass. It may be a short list, but it's more than most traditional Italian restaurants offer.

Right, to the food.

It's fine. It doesn't dazzle too much; it doesn't disappoint too often. It begins with excellent virgin olive oil, spiked with sun-dried tomatoes and chilli flakes, to accompany fresh white bread. The kitchen's strengths include a ripe, sparkling tomato sauce. This is the main reason the marriage of eggplant and cheese is so happy in the starter of melanzane Fiori, which rolls the svelte slices of eggplant around a filling of spinach and ricotta, topped but not smothered with mozzarella, baked and napped with that fine sauce. It bathes the house gnocchi too, the delicious dumplings paired with prosciutto and mushrooms, sharpened with Padano cheese.

I am offered ground pepper (of course) for the straciatella soup. I decline, as I tend to. Turns out to be a smart move, as the delicate, full-flavoured egg-drop soup has been assertively peppered in the kitchen. I like the simple starter of roasted red pepper, the skin charred and peeled away but the sweet roasted flavours intact in the flesh, each strip overlaid with a strip of anchovy, anointed with concentrated balsamic and good oil.

It's November, so we stay clear of the various salads that feature the tomato, choosing instead the lightly dressed greens strewn with charred artichokes (canned, but good) and thyme-flecked mushrooms. It is fine.

The house veal is rolled and stuffed with provolone, capocollo ham, spinach, and basil—all breaded, baked, and set in a sweet Marsala wine sauce. It's a comfort dish. From the pasta section, the ravioli Natasha is a letdown—the pasta pouches gummy and starchy, the lobster filling disagreeably fishy-tasting. For dessert, the ubiquitous tiramisu is delicious. The zabaglione I find too sweet—heavy with sugar in the yolks, not enough Marsala.

FIORI
239 Nepean St. (between Kent and Bank)
(613) 232-1377
www.fiorisrestaurant.com
Access: Three steps up to entrance; washrooms are on main level
Price: Main dishes $15 to $29
Open: Lunch Mon.-Fri.; dinner Mon.-Sat.; closed Sun.

FITZGERALD'S

★★★   **Contemporary**   **$$$**

Nick Diak and Brent Pattee aren't boys anymore, though at twenty-three they're still awfully close. And they've been close, these two, since their brown-tail days at Beavers. They went through primary school together, made the T-ball team together, and the Hopewell school band, on to football at Glebe Collegiate and then to chef school at Algonquin. Today, Diak and Pattee are working in close quarters in the open kitchen of Fitzgerald's, in this 150-year-old Victorian woolen mill in Almonte, surrounded with the art and merchandise of the Fitzgerald's store.

Their menu is compelling: it's short, for one, and uncontaminated by complicated ingredients or long-winded descriptions of preparation and pairing. There is a list of daily specials, from which we begin with the leek and sweet-potato soup, perfectly wonderful, of strong leek flavour, thick and rich with roasted puréed vegetable. And then warm, oozing Brie, studded with roasted pecans, served with a fruity confit of caramelized onions. The Caesar salad is a superior presentation of whole leaves of tender romaine, drizzled with a robust dressing, dotted with capers, croutons, bacon, and topped with shards of strong Parmesan. Mussels are the best I've had since a summer trip to P.E.I.: small, firm, and fresh, smothered in a rich, creamy pesto sauce. Not a dud in the lot of them.

From the list of specials, a thick hunk of sea bass stands out, the perfectly roasted fish set in a pale saffron sauce scented with dill. Five lamb chops, smeared with the classic garlic-mustard-rosemary mix, were perfectly medium-rare, reassuringly old-fashioned, and very good. They shared the plate with smashing mashed potatoes, a sweet potato purée accented with ginger, impeccable snap peas, roasted red peppers, and steamed broccoli.

We brought the meal to its conclusion with profiteroles and crème brûlée. The choux puffs tasted stale, but were filled with first-class ice cream and such a heavenly chocolate sauce, I could forgive the day-old baking. The crème brûlée was suitably rich and soothing, dressed up with a layer of raspberries—but you first had to contend with a crust that was too thick, too hard to crack, too sweet.

FITZGERALD'S

7 Mill St. (at Almonte St.)
Almonte
(613) 256-2524
Access: Fully accessible, including washrooms
Price: Main dishes $15 to $26
Open: Lunch Wed.-Fri.; dinner Wed.-Sun.; brunch Sat. and Sun.

FLYING PIGGY'S

★★   Italian $$

Looking for an affordable restaurant in which more-than-decent food is served by a kind crew in unpretentious surroundings? Not fussed about going to the corner of Bank Street and Heron Road to find it? Well, here you go. Look for the stout pig with pink wings airborne on a big brown sign—the only bit of animation at an otherwise tedious city intersection.

Flying Piggy's is a cosy space of bare wood floors, reddened walls, and densely packed tables. Halogen spots suspended on long black poles light up the hand-drawn murals, the various menu boards, and the pigs perched here, there, and everywhere.

Soups are one of this kitchen's strengths. A carrot purée is lightened with mango and peaches, spiced up with chilli, and fragrant with ginger, cinnamon, and cloves. It has a warm, rounded flavour that pleases to the last slurp. Fennel and cumin add smack to a bowl of steaming mussels bathed in garlic and wine, and pungent with black olives and capers—the last drops soaked up with good warm bread.

Pasta is homemade and properly cooked. The "Flighty Boar" allies fettucine with prosciutto, mushrooms, white wine, garlic, and cream. I found it wanting some green flavour (a chop of parsley, perhaps?) but otherwise a dandy plate of comfort on a snowy April night.

A fillet of fresh tuna is the special. It is ordered rare and it arrives rare. Its pepper-crusted surface is missing the promised grill flavour, but still this is a pleasant piece of fish, served atop a mound of braised greens and napped with a fine tarragon-scented butter sauce. The only truly sad bit of the meal is the veal. I've had

Flying Piggy's veal before and I've never been let down, but this go-round brought a piccata (with lemons and capers in a white wine sauce) that was tough and juiceless. Good whipped potatoes and the same pleasant sauté of vegetables finished the plate.

The featured crumble dessert—apples, pears, almonds, and ginger—sounded promising but was tasteless. A very, very fine pecan pie, dense with nuts and sweet with maple syrup, was the hit.

FLYING PIGGY'S
1665 Bank St. (between Heron and Alta Vista)
(613) 526-4900
Access: One step into restaurant; three steps up to washrooms
Prices: Main dishes $9.50 to $25.95
Open: Lunch Mon.-Fri.; dinner daily

FRATELLI IN KANATA

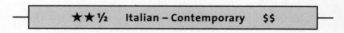

★★½   Italian – Contemporary $$

Tucked away at the end of one of Kanata's interminable mall monstrosities is an unexpectedly good place to eat. The Valente brothers, who brought us the original Fratelli on Bank Street, have taken their menu and their interior decorator west, with fine results.

Notwithstanding its strip-mall exterior, this is a good-looking restaurant. If you know the Glebe Fratelli, the look will seem familiar—here too are the soaring ceilings, the exposed brick wall, the large oval mirrors, and the rich, splendid colours. Here too is the whimsical collection of old black-and-white family photographs. The elements of the room are attractively balanced and the materials—from the comfortable wooden chairs to the ceiling-to-floor wine rack—seem top-of-the-line.

The menu at Fratelli in Kanata is also familiar—similar, if not identical, to the one on Bank. You can't go wrong with a Caesar salad, treated with a robust dressing that takes on more life with a squeeze of lemon, topped with slices of crisp pancetta and shards of good Parmesan. Big shrimp, soft scallops, and rings of squid are served cold, anointed simply with lemon and olive oil and presented in a radicchio "cup." At dinner, the squid are yielding beneath their crisp, thyme-flecked batter, judiciously fried and served with a homemade tartare sauce. The nutty-flavoured prosciutto from Parma is fanned onto a plate of young greens, strong with arugula, and complemented by a fruity apple-and-fresh-fig chutney. The distinction of the house carpaccio is the horseradish mustard sauce and the slivers of hard Parmesan with which the red fresh-cut beef tenderloin is strewn.

It's not all sunshine and light. The salmon is overcooked, though rescued somewhat by its pleasant pineapple and mango sauce that's perfumed with cilantro and garnished with deep-fried "leaves" of garlic and leek. The roasted chicken breast, stuffed with prosciutto, spinach, and goat cheese, has the flavour of a happy chicken, but the meat is drier than we like. The gnocchi are not as light as they should be, and the tomato basil sauce tastes too much like cream and tomato paste and not enough like fresh tomatoes and basil. So it's the rack of lamb that racks up all the points: roasted to ruby perfection with a crust of rosemary, mustard, and chopped pecans and a dark sauce strong of lamb jus, wine, and pepper, served with a full complement of faultless vegetables.

Fratelli's crème brûlée is rich and creamy — more pudding-like than is strictly correct, but the flavour is quite wonderful and the overall effect is totally soothing.

The Fratelli wine list is extensive, with many Italian offerings but also with a good number of bottles from the New World. A generous selection is available by the glass or half-litre.

FRATELLI IN KANATA
499 Terry Fox Dr. (at Campeau)
Kanata
(613) 592-0225
Original Fratelli is at 749 Bank St. (at First) (613) 237-1658
Access: Fully wheelchair accessible
Price: Pizza, pasta, and main dishes $10 to $23
Open: Lunch Mon.-Fri.; dinner Mon.-Sun.

GIOVANNI'S

★★★   Italian – Traditional $$$

All right, I'll admit it. The plethora of foyer photos of famous people, arms draped around the Giovanni owners, gave me instamatic unhappy preconceptions. Was this self-important little place to be about fashion or food? Service to the known, or hospitality for all? I had some time to examine the pictures and muse. My table wasn't quite ready. It was a Tuesday night, freezing rain, and Giovanni's was packed with a waiting queue out the door.

Once the table service began and the food appeared, the appeal of this place became clear. Ottawa may be studded with traditional Italian restaurants of this quality, but perhaps none are quite so fine as Giovanni's.

What the place does particularly well is not skimp on the number of waitstaff. There are half a dozen black-trousered gents in blue work shirts, all on high alert to the needs of the two small rooms. "Our" server knew his job. He knew the wine list, knew the menu, knew when to show, when to go.

He brought foie gras to start, bless him, browned and crusted, soft and succulent, set on a layer of fleshy oyster mushrooms. Beneath the quivering foie and the mushrooms was a thick-cut slice of bread, fried in olive oil and butter and then on top, napping the lot, was an elegant sauce of wine, cream, and liver-y pan juices. It was rich as hell and costly, but if they've got this starter on the menu, order it. Skip dessert.

If not, start lightly with soup. Giovanni's chicken broth has glorious flavour. Try it enriched with a lightly poached egg, a round of garlic toast and a dollop of roasted red pepper aioli. Or perhaps a salad of many textures and flavours: salty anchovies, pungent garlic, and soft sweet strips of roasted red pepper set on a bitter bed of radicchio, slightly wilted under a warm balsamic-and-olive-oil anointment.

There is an appetizer portion of gnocchi on this menu, so delicate the dumplings barely hold their shape, set in a flavourful sauce of ripe tomatoes and fresh basil.

That same ripe tomato sauce gives depth to the cannelloni, the pasta house-made and perfectly al dente, the stuffing of veal, herbs, spinach, and ricotta light and packed with flavour. Giovanni's veal Marsala is the classic, the sauce boozy and sweet, the meat pounded, tender, toothsome. Chicken medaillons shine under a vigorous tomato sauce spiced with hot peppers and black olives. Perfect roast potatoes, green beans, carrots, and cauliflower finish the dish.

Good risotto here: dense with porcini mushrooms, the rice soft-ened but the centre of the grains still al dente, this dish is just the right degree of creamy. The only false move is the overcooked veal chop, otherwise fine with its sautéed oyster mushroom covering and its accompaniment of just-wilted spinach zinged with lemon and garlic.

We opt for zabaglione to close, in lieu of the tired-looking cakes displayed on a platter. The sweet boozy froth disappears on the tongue.

And while I'm niggling: a restaurant that brings lemon for the water and switches crystal wine glasses to match the bottle should not serve butter in paper packets. And service that's been top-notch all evening should not tire at the end, leaving us to fetch our own coats from the back hall. You were kind enough to remove my coat when I arrived; you may fetch it for me when I leave.

A final note on the wine list: it is lengthy, and clearly a priority here.

GIOVANNI'S

362 Preston St. (at Aberdeen)
(613) 234-3156
www.giovannis-restaurant.com
Access: One step from street level; washrooms are small
Price: Main dishes $12 to $45
Open: Lunch Mon.-Fri.; dinner daily

GOJO

★★   **Ethiopian** $

Fermented pancakes the size of dinner napkins are our plates—five of them are draped over a large tin tray. On these are little mounds of earth-coloured stews—shades of brown, some mellow yellow, a disquieting scorched red. These are the various "watts"—stewed meats, vegetables, grains—of a traditional Ethiopian meal. And these are the offerings at Gojo, a recent addition to the smattering of Ethiopian restaurants in this city, located in a small brick house bounded by the strip malls and gas stations of a busy section of Bank Street.

No cutlery is provided on these bare tables. For the uninitiated, photographs on the back of the Gojo menu give you hand-by-hand instructions. It all begins with the napkin-sized "plates." If you've never tried these, you're in for a spongy treat. Fashioned out of teff, a tiny millet-like grain unique to Ethiopia (and *loaded* with iron—women, take note) this pancake-like bread is called injera. It has a pleasant sourdough flavour and literally underlies every Ethiopian meal.

You eat communally, sharing one big platter. Start by tearing off a small piece of injera and, with the fingers and thumb of the right hand (the Ethiopian custom) use it to pinch and scoop up bits of the mounds. Some of the dollops are fiercely spicy, some are meek and mild; all are intensely fragrant. A plate of fresh injera arrives just as you think you've had it with all the tearing and the scooping and the sampling. And so you start again.

The delicately seasoned watts are called "alicha." Their exotic flavour has much to do with "miter kebben," a clarified and flavoured butter with which the meat or vegetable is cooked. Should you wish to add some intensity to the more subtle stews, there is berbere, Ethiopia's aromatic but haunting red pepper paste.

Start with the mild and work your way toward the red: to stews like the fiery "key" watt (slightly chewy beef simmered in a complex sauce that includes berbere) or the "yemesir" watt (lentils in an aromatic sauce of substantial clout). There is the Ethiopian version of steak tartare, kitfo, which is chopped fillet, raw or very slightly cooked, rich with seasoned butter. We order ours uncooked, a mound of rather coarsely-handled meat—some of it minced, some of it chopped, none of it particularly refined, but all of it tasty—to which you may add more of the dried spice mix called mittmita . . . or leave it alone. We found more oomph, in moderation, suited us.

There are no starters, other than a refreshing salad of bouncy-fresh greens, with ripe tomatoes, pickled onion, and a simple but rousing dose of lemon, oil, and sliced green chillies.

The drinks list disappoints. I was hoping for some Ethiopian-style beer or honey wine (tej). Instead, there's a bit of wine and the usual brews, along with soft drinks. There's scented tea (chai), though; and with two days' warning, a traditional Ethiopian coffee service can be arranged—in which Ethiopian beans are hand-roasted, ground, steeped, and served with ceremony in a cosy room upstairs.

The service is kind and keen but not in any hurry. If you are, best warn the management.

GOJO
1542 Bank St. (at Evans)
(613) 737-0550
Access: Stairs into restaurant; washrooms are upstairs
Price: Main dishes $6 to $11
Open: Lunch Tues.-Sat.; dinner Tues.-Sun.; closed Mon.

GOOD FOOD CO.

★★   Café $

Carleton Place is blessed with this little gem. The Good Food Co. is a cheery orange space of two dozen mismatched wooden chairs, a large take-away counter, and excellent home cooked comfort food. Chemistry major Petra Graber—whose background may explain why the desserts are so delicious—is the owner and cook.

The short weekly menu leans in all kinds of wacky directions. One week, we tuck into a coconut milk curry of shredded chicken and vegetables, fragrant with ginger, cardamom, and cumin, served with couscous and mango chutney. Next visit brings fresh shrimp cooked in a rich red sauce of plum tomato, olives, basil, feta, and garlic, served with steamed rice and a salad.

There are full-flavoured soups here, big bouncy salads, and desserts to ditch the diet for: a whisky-spiked pound cake is moist and boozy, and lemon trifle is served with lemon cream and fresh local berries. Ginger cookies come with the cappuccinos.

The Good Food Co. service is reliably cheerful and, if you come on the right Saturday night, there's live music. The wine list is short—five reds, five whites, all available by the glass. But if you don't book one of the batik-covered tables, you'll be dining on hot dogs at the bowling alley down the block.

GOOD FOOD CO.
31 Bridge St.
Carleton Place
(613) 257-7284
Access: Two steps into restaurant; washrooms are small
Price: Main dishes $9 to $15
Open: Breakfast and lunch Tues.-Wed. and Sun.; breakfast, lunch, and dinner Thurs.-Sat.; closed Mon.

GRAFFITI'S

★★   **Mediterranean** $$

Adding "Select" to the name of a Holiday Inn may seem like attempting to "spin" a Big Mac into a sirloin. But Graffiti's, the dining room of the Holiday Inn "Select," is trying to break out of the typical please-'em-all continental-bland hotel restaurant. And it's largely succeeding. They've got a look, a style, a pizza oven, and a fun bar. For Kanata, desperate for decent dining rooms, that's more than sufficient.

It's a big sunny room with high ceilings, gleaming wood, commodious banquettes, and a handsome, soaring bar. The kitchen is more or less open, and the pizza oven anchors the show. The menu is modern Italian, with much of the what-you'd-expect stuff—and some quite interesting surprises as well, such as osso bucco as part of the regular menu.

The regular menu also includes gazpacho, a chilled seasonal soup not worth eating out of season. In March, we sampled instead the "zuppa del giorno," a seafood bisque strong of salmon, with clear seafood flavour, and nicely seasoned. The mixed greens were bouncy-fresh, tossed with a pleasant balsamic vinaigrette. We liked the grilled calamari appetizer, tender and toothsome, drizzled with reduced balsamic vinegar and garnished with a julienne of leeks and carrot. Fine too was the shrimp starter, firm and sweet in their rich bath of cream and sambuca, littered with snips of chive and tiny cubes of still-crunchy carrot. The Caesar salad, however, was not a spectacular version, and the mussels were too fishy-tasting in a banal tomato sauce.

The pizza comes from the wood-fired oven, its thin crust crisp in the right spots, chewy in others, and covered with fresh, respectable toppings (tomatoes, olives, feta, fresh basil).

For a hotel restaurant to cook bang-on pasta is impressive. Graffiti's linguine all'olio featured those perfectly al dente noodles tossed lightly with good olive oil, sweetly roasted garlic, fresh parsley, basil, a tiny dice of red pepper, and a good sprinkling of freshly grated parmigiano.

Of the main dishes, two impressed. The veal was tender meat, the Frangelico cream sauce pleasant (if you like sweet and rich), all of it dotted with toasted pine nuts. The aged tenderloin was fine, the meat seared on the outside, juicy on the inside, brushed with butter and topped with a dollop of Gorgonzola. But it was a small portion and, though good, not $29 good. The final main dish was chicken, stuffed with prosciutto, provolone, and basil, but sadly, badly dry and juiceless.

The crème caramel was too cold and the tiramisu was pretty ordinary. The cappuccino, however, was excellent.

GRAFFITI'S
Holiday Inn Select
101 Kanata Ave. (at Lord Byng)
(613) 271-0921
www.graffitis.ca/kanata
Access: Fully wheelchair accessible
Price: Pizza, pasta, and main dishes $12 to $26.75
Open: Daily for breakfast, lunch, and dinner

GREEN PAPAYA

★★ ½   Thai $$

If you're looking for the what-you'd-expect lineup of Thai "favou-rites," well executed, served sweetly, enjoyed in vibrant crimson surroundings, the Green Papaya is a good choice.

Here you'll find the standard repertoire of classic Thai soups, sear-ing salads, stir-fries, curries, rice, and noodle dishes. If you want a fifty-dollar bill to cover your meal, here's what you order: two bowls of aromatic tom yum, two main dishes—stir-fried pork with fresh chilli and basil and, for the real adventurer, wild bamboo curry with chicken—add a bowl of rice, a pot of lemongrass tea, and hooray for you, you've done it.

It's the starters that spike the bill. But they're hard to resist.

Complimentary shrimp chips and peanut dipping sauce arrive thirty seconds after the Singha beer. Two minutes later, soup. We stick our noses right into the bowl and sniff up those glorious smells—still exotic after all these years of getting to know the flavours and aromas of Thai cuisine.

The chicken saté is tender, fragrant meat, and spicier than you'll find served elsewhere. Tod mun pla are fish cakes, yielding, moist, presented with strips of cucumber for crunchy contrast and a too-sweet chilli sauce for dunking. That chilli sauce is a recurring theme. It shows up again with #4: kai yadd sai are two fat chicken wings, boned, stuffed with ground pork and cellophane noodles, perfectly fried to golden, moist, meaty perfection. It also shows up with the poh pia goong tod, in which two crunchy shrimp are encased in spring- roll wrappers and fried to crisp.

Squid is chopped, marinated, grilled, and served with the same impressive peanut sauce that comes with the saté.

If you're weary of pad Thai, switch to the racier pad ki mow: wide noodles with egg, scallion, Thai basil, red-hot chilli peppers and the meat of your choice. The three-chilli-pepper symbol next to the listing for this dish is to be minded.

The citrus zing of lime leaves, the heat of red chillies and the comfort of coconut milk are the bold contrasts the panaeng curry offers.

There's nothing dreary about the décor here. The Green Papaya is a very pretty, tamarind-orange room, its ceiling crossed with thick wooden beams painted white, its walls covered in Thai art and artifacts, ornate mirrors, antique statues.

There's a sweet little room off to one side that can fit four people. That's where a baby was seated on a crazy busy Friday night, joining in the noisiness of a bustling, happy room.

GREEN PAPAYA
260 Nepean St. (at Kent)
(613) 231-8424
www.greenpapaya.ca
Access: Steps into restaurant; washrooms are downstairs
Price: Main dishes $9.50 to $16.95
Open: Lunch Mon.-Fri.; daily for dinner

HAVELI

★★   Indian $$

Except for the few luxury ingredients you find on it (fresh lobster, sea scallops, leg of lamb), the Haveli menu is much the same as that of any other Indian restaurant in this city. The same deep-fried packages start you off, the ubiquitous mulligatawny soup is here, as is the long list of items from the tandoor. There are half a dozen basmati rice dishes, the usual selection of fragrant Indian breads, and various curries that roam the subcontinent but mostly look to the Punjab for preparation style.

Haveli's assets also include spacious comfort, glass-enclosed tandoor ovens and (except when there's a big birthday party in full swing) an ambience of quiet elegance.

Cumin-studded pappadum arrive, on the house. And then a spicy sambar to shake up our mouths, the broth thick with lentils, plump with vegetables, fragrant with spices, sweet and sour with tamarind, and fired up with green chillies. The naan is quite wonderful. The mussels are not—overcooked, fishy-tasting, and in a broth that's loud with cream and raw curry powder.

Yogurt soothes and a tamarind sauce excites a starter of potato topped with a fragrant chickpea curry. The seekh kebab is moist and aromatic of coriander. We prefer it to the ho-hum "brown" starters—the onion bhaji, the samosas, and the battered shrimp.

I find, as I often do, that vegetarian dishes appeal more. We try the slow-simmered grainy dhal, greened with spinach and layered with flavour. The red-brown sauce around the tandoor-roasted baigan bharta furthers the cause of those of us who believe that eggplant—in the hands of one who knows how to show it off—is one of the world's great vegetables.

The vegetable biryani is not particularly distinctive. The bland, overcooked vegetables add nothing much; the rice seems cooked a while ago. Better the plain rice, dotted with sweetly fried onion, that tastes just-steamed, each grain separate, fluffy, nutty-smelling. That rice comes on the side of an intensely seasoned but sadly dried-out leg of lamb. The side of caramelized onion and wedges of cumin-scented roast potato helps matters, but clearly this meat has seen the inside of the tandoor earlier and has suffered in its reheating.

The wonderful sour hit is here, as is the nutty taste and dark co-lour, but the searing heat of an authentic Gao vindaloo is not fully realized. This is not a criticism so much as a thank-you. I love the pucker of a good vindaloo, but cannot tolerate the excessive chilli heat. The chunks of beef in Haveli's version are very tender, the gravy is rich and fragrant, and the dried red chillies can be worked around (or through), depending on your affection for them. The butter chicken suffers, though, from tough meat and too much cream. The subtle spicing is overwhelmed in this delicate dish. Nothing tough about the shrimp, though; a generous quantity of good-sized ones are fresh tasting and perfectly cooked in a bhoona preparation with tomato, onion, and a jumble of spices.

There are rose- and cardamom-scented Indian desserts, for which you require a sweet tooth, and a decent mango cheesecake. The pistachio-sprinkled ras malai, poached balls of fresh cream cheese set in a luscious, milky, highly perfumed sauce, are fresh and inter-esting. You either love them or you don't.

HAVELI
39 Clarence St. (near Sussex)
(613) 241-1700
www.haveli.com
Also located in Bells Corners, 194 Robertson Rd. (close to Moody)
(613) 820-1700
Access: Steps into restaurant; washrooms are downstairs
Price: Main dishes $7.50 to $39.95
Open: Brunch/lunch Sun.-Fri.; dinner daily.; closed Sat. lunch.

HO HO

★ ★ ½   Chinese $

I don't know if the balloons have been a part of the experience for all the twenty-four years that Ho Ho's has been dishing out the chow mein, but they sure were a hit at my table. They arrived with the bill and the fortune cookies. And not just any old balloons—these were blown up tableside, twisted into swords for the lads, and followed up with an invitation to go joust (that is, whack each other) in an adjoining, empty, apparently sword-proof dining room. Meanwhile, the bill got paid, the leftovers got packaged up, and the last gulps of the Tsing Tao beers were taken in peace.

If I tell you I believe Ho Ho's may be the best family restaurant in Ottawa, I'll be spoiling everything. The place is a private pleasure for my gang and, for our dining-out-with-the-kids dollar, it's a treasure. My plan here is to broadcast my enthusiasm for this place, but only if you promise not to go.

Which is not to say that Ho Ho's is a well-kept secret. Folks have been coming here—to Richmond Road east of Woodroffe—for over twenty years, sometimes from far afield. Before that, they went to the Ho Ho's in Lincoln Fields, which was a small take-away spot.

Our family first came for ice cream. It was the après-soccer treat: a chocolate dip cone from the ice-cream stand in the Chinese restaurant's parking lot. We'd sit at the picnic tables, lick the drips, swat the wasps, and watch the traffic. The restaurant was about ice cream, we thought, not egg rolls.

When we finally did venture in, we were hooked. Ho Ho's is not a posh spot. And the menu—apart from being colourful and thoughtfully laid out—does not distinguish itself from any other "dine-in, take-out, we deliver" Chinese restaurant. But the food is fresh, the vegetables offer more than the usual bean sprouts and bok choy, the chicken has real chicken flavour, the beef is tender, the shrimp crunchy, the sauces have life, and none of it has MSG. The other joy of this place is the Ho family running it: they're gracious, amusing, and good fun.

My favourite dish (and one I have all to myself, as the lads can think of nothing more revolting) is the enormous sizzling platter of shrimp-stuffed Chinese eggplant smothered in black bean sauce. The eggplant arrive lonely on the cast-iron platter and then the black bean sauce is poured over their deep purple skins tableside with great sizzle and smoke (*this* they like). The sauce is pungent, spicy, a fine match for the soft-spoken eggplant. The shrimp within are sweet, crunchy, perfect.

Ho Ho's does a very fine ginger-beef too — the meat lean and remarkably tender, the ginger flavour strong, the onions caramelized, the sauce with just the right amount of bite. The lads like the sweet and sour spare ribs, with peppers and pineapple, the ribs coated with that glorious, memory-making, cornstarch-thickened, sweet reddened sauce.

The mo-shu anything (beef, pork, chicken) is popular here: tender meat, softly cooked egg, vegetables, Chinese mushrooms, all available to wrap up in a "tissue pancake" and dunk in hoisin sauce. The boys also like the won ton soup, the chicken chow mein and any of the spring rolls (shrimp, vegetable, chicken).

For a family of six, we paid about $100, with two Tsing Taos, four root beer, balloons on the house, and a spare room facilitating a moment of adult peace.

HO HO
875 Richmond Rd. (east of Woodroffe)
(613) 722-9200
www.hohochinesefood.com
Access: Two steps into restaurant
Price: Main dishes $7 to $15
Open: Lunch Tues.-Fri.; dinner Tues.-Sun.; closed Mon.

IL PICCOLINO

★★   Italian $$

The patio at Il Piccolino is sheltered from the bustle of Preston Street traffic by a thick vine-wrapped arbour. Right now, in summer, it's green and lush with leaves. In a few weeks it'll be dripping purple with grapes. On a balmy evening, the dozen tables are full. If you haven't booked your shaded place in the sun, you're going inside — to one of the ten tables stuffed in this quaint old house.

There is much busyness in the homespun green, red, and white décor. Black-and-whites of family in the old country line the rough walls.

The dull white bread in the basket is worrying. So are the rubbery, fishy rings of squid, bare but for the lemon wedge, with none of the sizable, oily anointment promised. Better to start with a salad — they make a fine Caesar here. The "insalata rustica" is a big plate of well-roasted vegetables (zucchini, peppers, garlic) and oozy warm goat cheese perched on greens, dressed with a summery, fruity vinaigrette.

Or why not go for the quintessential comfort food: mushrooms on toast, simmered with wine, garlic, cream, thick with parsley, and dotted with a wee dice of carrot for colour and crunch. Just-grated Parmesan caps the generous mushroom mound.

Pasta, as you'd expect, has a prominent place on this menu, as does pizza. Both are good. You will enjoy the marriana, the large round ravioli perfectly al dente, stuffed with ricotta, chopped artichoke hearts, well-roasted peppers, and bathed in a lightly creamed tomato sauce dotted with whole cloves of caramelized garlic.

Four pizzas are offered, plus a daily special. The toppings are sensible (no kiwi); the crust chewy in the right places, soft in others, sweet throughout, spread with a rich tomato base.

The chicken breast is stuffed tastily with toasted pine nuts. But although it's moistened with sautéed leeks and a fine cider cream sauce, the chicken flesh remains dry and juiceless.

The house tiramisu is a gem, the delicate balance of cake-mascarpone-cream-booze-coffee right on.

Two dozen wines make up the list. They are mostly Italian, but some well-known New World wines are represented too. The bottles range in price from $22 to $50.

IL PICCOLINO
449 Preston St. (at Pamilla)
(613) 236-8158
www.ilpiccolino.ca
Access: Steps into restaurant and down to washrooms;
summer patio is accessible
Price: Main dishes $16 to $19
Open: Lunch Mon.-Fri.; dinner daily

IL PRIMO

★★   **Italian** $$

Il Primo, like its big sister Il Piccolino down the road, offers tasty, fresh food, civilized service, and value for the dining-out dollar. Il Piccolino, the more casual of the two, offers mainly pasta and pizza. Il Primo has the white linen. And nothing is baked on a crust.

Dark panelling and rich Mediterranean colours fill the L-shaped interior. A half-dozen stools flank a good-looking bar. The floors are ceramic; the walls are wood in places, pale caramel in others, with blue and yellow trim. In the evening, the soft spotlights and candles create an inviting intimacy.

A carafe of water is left on the table. The white wine arrives with a cooler. The bread basket is passed often. We enjoy the thoughtful service.

For those to whom a good Caesar salad is critical, this one features fresh romaine, a lively dressing, garlic-rubbed croutons, and good Parmesan. But the spinach salad is better: the leaves are layered with marinated artichokes, softened dried apricots, and chunks of Cambozola cheese, and the lot is anointed with a warm balsamic-sesame oil vinaigrette.

Here is Cambozola again, chunks of the rich, blue-veined cheese meltingly good in a thick bowl of roasted and puréed carrot. At lunch, we're crazy for the vegetable sandwich: it's served on foccacia bread, with roasted strips of eggplant, zucchini, onion, treated with a fragrant layer of pesto, and quite wonderful with a smoked mozzarella cover.

Olives, capers, and garlic dominate the piquant tomato sauce that bathes the plump Primo mussels. Another pleasurable starter is the rotelle: prosciutto rolled around bocconcini cheese and figs, warmed in an Alfredo sauce strong of garlic. The one that fails to impress is the polenta with cheese; the browned cornmeal is dry, bland, covered with a stiff layer of provolone.

A more-than-decent farfalle from the pasta section has the firm bow ties coated in a rich pesto of oil, basil, almonds, and lemon zest, mingled with strips of red and green peppers and moist, properly grilled shrimp. Less exciting is the manicotti, which suffers from undercooked pasta. Problems too with the pork — sliced and pounded tenderloin is overdone and dry, although helped by a good sauce of reduced pork juices splashed with balsamic vinaigrette and perfumed with fresh basil. The risotto that comes with it is slightly undercooked.

Back to form for the finale: a dessert crêpe of ricotta cheese with berries benefits from the sweetness of a bath in crème anglaise. A chocolate amaretto cheesecake is dreamy.

A thoughtfully assembled, user-friendly wine list is notable for its international focus. The Italian section is longest, but Canada, Australia, France, and California each get a piece of it.

IL PRIMO

371 Preston St. (at Beech)
(613) 234-6858
www.ilprimo.ca
Access: Steps into restaurant from street level
Price: Pasta and main dishes $11.95 to $17.95
Open: Lunch Mon.-Fri; dinner Mon.-Sun.

IL VAGABONDO

★★   Italian $$

Il Vagabondo is a modest Italian restaurant found, if you're paying attention, on a skinny side street just off the Beechwood Avenue restaurant row. On a quiet night, when chef/owner Adriana Roy emerges from her kitchen, her big smile lights up the place. When she's too busy to socialize, the staff takes over, sometimes sweet-natured—but sometimes not. I've had both.

What I've never had was a disappointing meal. I like Roy's formula: homemade pasta of your choice with the sauce of your choice. Reads like cafeteria options, but with sauces that shine on home-made, properly cooked pasta, the results are splendid. Then there's the best lasagna in town, meltingly good gnocchi, remarkably tender veal, fresh salmon with a green sauce, and a fine grilled steak smothered with onions and peppers. I like her prices too: incredibly modest. As for the environment, it's homey, simple, fine.

Order the house zucchini; you'll forget all about those greasy, soggy, stringy commercial sticks you scarf down in pubs. These are light, flavourful, crunchy gems—addictively good. Two soups are on offer: a summer bowl of gazpacho, slightly fired-up, and a bittersweet leek soup, fleshed out with watercress, made with a well-flavoured broth. The carpaccio is sliced to order, the thin, ruby peels of loin boosted with lemon, capers, olives, and sharp parmigiano.

There are mussels, a big bowl of them as a starter course, steamed to just-open in a wine and herb broth. You find them too in the noodle special—along with fresh sea scallops, chunks of juicy salmon and crunchy-sweet shrimp, all mingled with delicate fettuccine in a fragrant tomato sauce.

A dozen layers of the thinnest, most dainty sheets of pasta are napped lightly with a flavour-rich veal sauce sparkling with basil. That's the lasagna al Vagabondo, the best $14 you'll ever spend.

There are eight ways with veal. Our way had the fork-tender, pounded-thin meat bathed in a buttery sauce piqued with anchovies, olives, tomatoes, and herbs.

A cinnamon-infused crème caramel is overcooked. A buttery home-made cake is better, topped with fresh pineapple and soaked in rum. The wine list is ho-hum. The espresso is excellent.

IL VAGABONDO
186 Barette St. (at Marrier, off Beechwood)
(613) 749-4877
Access: Steps into restaurant; washrooms are small
Price: Main dishes $11 to $26
Open: Lunch Tues.-Fri.; dinner Tues.-Sun.

JAPANESE VILLAGE

★★   Japanese $$$

Located forever in the basement of a downtown office tower, the Japanese Village is a large, dark, dated-looking space that offers the basic sushi-tempura-teriyaki fare with the bonus spectacle of the teppanyaki.

We were three women come to watch a man cook us dinner. Perched around the teppanyaki grill, we had a very funny fellow with big knives and a fondness for pyrotechnics all to ourselves.

He's not cooking us much that's exotic — surf and turf with a splash of teriyaki, sizzled up with plenty of pizzazz. It's great fun for kids, for birthdays, for celebrations when the food's important, but perhaps not so much as the show.

Prior to the performance, we ordered sushi from the set menu. These were firm, clean-tasting rice snacks, roused with the usual stuff. An appetizer portion of tempura was not the ultimate, but its batter was light enough and free of grease, coating shrimp that were sweet and vegetables that were crisp.

Our main dishes came with shabu shabu soup (pleasant), a "village" salad (made of iceberg lettuce and unremarkable), yaki shrimp (fresh, bouncy shrimp seared with ginger and soy), Japanese rice, and green tea.

Cups of warm sake in hand, we braced ourselves for the fire and light. It began with "Japanese" mushrooms (strictly button) fired up with butter and soy sauce and lots of chatter from our chef. Next, a platter of sea scallops, a duck breast, and a sirloin steak, escorted by various squeeze bottles of secret sauces, wedges of orange and lemon, all lined up and ready for action. The duck went first, grilled to rare, treated with a splash of teriyaki sauce and a squeeze of orange, thinly sliced and tasting supple and moist. The steak received a sesame sauce finish; the scallops were bathed in a ginger sauce. All of it was good. None of it was remarkable.

What *is* remarkable is the show, the chatter, the fire, the flying food, and the wide eyes of the children in the room.

JAPANESE VILLAGE

170 Laurier Ave. West (at Metcalfe)
(613) 236-9519
www.japanesevillage.net
Access: Restaurant in basement; an elevator is available; washrooms are accessible
Price: Complete meals from $16 to $32
Open: Lunch Tues.-Fri.; dinner Tues.-Sun.; closed Mon.

JUNIPER KITCHEN & WINE BAR

★★★★   Contemporary $$$$

In a neighbourhood that seems to be constantly changing, Juniper remains steadily planted. Which is not to suggest that this Westboro restaurant is rigid or complacent. It's always changing, too, at least to the extent of the new dishes regularly dreamed up by chefs/ owners Richard Nigro and Michael Sobcov.

Juniper has been one of Ottawa's top tables since it opened in 1996, showcasing the pure flavours and innovative combinations of contemporary, market-driven cooking. The confidence and success in experimentation here are grounded in solid technique and discipline. The results on the plate are delicious.

As for its physical space, Juniper is one of those uncluttered, modishly plain, mature-looking places some find stark, others find refreshing. Rather depends on your taste. But the food, the wine list, and the service—these are all in good taste.

A fall purée of roasted parsnip and apple is a smooth, flavour-rich, well-peppered soup, crowned with matchsticks of Granny Smith. Three plump mussels top a southwestern gumbo thick with tomato, okra, and celery, lively with chillies.

The kitchen rolls an oval ball of soft, fresh buffalo-milk mozzarella in toasted crushed hazelnuts, and balances the creamy richness with a marmalade tarted up with cranberries and apples. And on the side, just for fun, a mound of plantain frites. I remember crab cakes from an earlier visit here; rich, fragrant, and perfectly moist, served with a trio of dips including a homemade mayonnaise threaded with saffron.

There's a sure hand with fish at Juniper. Sushi-grade tuna is treated with ginger and sesame, grilled to rare, the moist, firm fish set on wilted spinach and supplied with two curry sauces: one a spicy green, the other a pale orange, pungent with mustard seed. The salt-crusted, deep brown surface of an excellent piece of beef is radiant red inside, its juices mingling with those of the wild mushrooms served alongside and pooling over lumpy mashed potatoes beneath.

The lunch menu lists a "grilled cheese sandwich." Somehow, you suspect it is an adult affair. Indeed: on herbed and salted foccaccia, smoked mozzarella is fortified with a black olive tapenade and slabs of sweetly grilled peppers and smoky eggplant. *That* kind of grilled cheese.

The standout dessert is a ridiculously awesome gingerbread cake with mascarpone cream. Runner-up is the classic crème brûlée, a cool, rich custard with a warm, thin, and gently crackling caramelized shell—no tampering with its pure flavour, thank you.

Juniper's wine list has been recognized with a Wine Spectator Award of Excellence for its collection of New World wines, focusing on California, Australia, and (increasingly) on Canada.

JUNIPER KITCHEN & WINE BAR
1293 Wellington St. West (west of Holland)
(613) 728-0220
Access: Small step at entrance; washrooms are downstairs
Price: Table d'hôte $30 to $44
Open: Lunch Tues.-Fri.; dinner Tues.-Sun.; closed Mon.

KASBAH VILLAGE

★★   Moroccan $$

The Kasbah Village's version of bestilla is perfumed with saffron and orange-blossom water. The cinnamon is potent, the filling fragrant and moist, the pie clearly made to order. A German dining companion, experiencing Moroccan food for the first time, took a bite and shrieked. This sugar-dusted, perfumed chicken pie was a horror for her.

In North African cooking, sugar is not confined to the dessert trolley. It is considered a flavouring like any other, a principal ingredient used in dishes some might consider strictly savoury. The line between fruits and vegetables is also blurred. Vegetables are often used in sweet chutneys, and dried and fresh fruits flavour fish and meat dishes, their natural sugars permeating the stew.

But not all is sweet. Harira, Morocco's national soup and basic staple, is made with lamb, chickpeas, lentils, vegetables, spices, often served with a side dish of harisa (peppery hot sauce). At the Kasbah Village, it is a tasty bowl, pungent with ginger, coriander, and pepper.

All savoury too is the tagine "Tangerois" of tender chicken, cooked with salt-preserved lemons (indispensable in Moroccan cuisine), briny green olives, potatoes, onions, saffron, and coriander. A second tagine provides a stark contrast: chicken again, tender again, but this time cooked with prunes, pears, pineapple, ginger, cinnamon, roasted almonds, and toasted sesame seeds, all adding significant sweetness to the sauce.

A side order of couscous is a meal-in-itself portion of the semolina grains, perfectly steamed with saffron and raisins, mounded up with chickpeas and seven vegetables—carrots, celery, two kinds of squash, zucchini, onion, and turnip.

For dessert, we steer clear of pastry treats and opt for oranges, sliced and bathed in a rosewater bath, dusted with cinnamon, topped with crushed pistachios. Our host, the charming Khalid Bouazza, pours our mint tea with ceremony and from great height into decorative glasses.

There is a decent Moroccan house wine to match this food.

KASBAH VILLAGE
261 Laurier Ave. (at O'Connor)
(613) 232-3737
Access: Fully accessible
Price: Main dishes $10.50 to $16.95
Open: Lunch daily; dinner Tues.-Sat.; closed Sun.

KINKI

★★½   Asian – Fusion $$$

Kinki's brand of Asian-fusion-sushi eats very well. They've hired a collection of servers who may be photogenic, but are also smart, polite, and good servers. The music is vibrant, the look is striking, and the guys who work the busy sushi bar are a friendly, smiley bunch. It's an attractive, animated, jolly place, open until one in the morning on the more happening nights. And when I turn fifty, I plan to book the big comfy couch at the back of the room, eat a grotesque amount of sushi, and ask the nice Kinki people to please turn down the music.

Even in my forties, I'm still not likely Kinki's target diner. At the risk of sounding square, I'll say it anyway: the music here can be intrusive. It pulses. And it seems to get louder and pulsier as the evening swells. By nine o'clock, I feel like I'm in a dance bar, not a restaurant.

If you head toward the striking painting of frolicking koi at the back of the main room, you'll find the sushi bar. Here they manufacture the dozens of varieties of sticky rice snacks, arranged on blocks of wood, prettied-up with deep purple basil.

It's easy to overeat this stuff. (It's also easy to run up quite a bill.) We did both. We started with an order of Kinki moriawase, the chef's choice of glistening fish draped over vinegared rice. This was followed with some yummy unorthodox stuff: "Kinki maki," featuring tuna, salmon, shrimp, and tamago (Japanese omelette), protected with rice, nori, and sesame, dipped in a light tempura batter and jump-fried until the coating puffs, the nori crackles, the sesame toasts, and the rice is slightly warm, while the raw fish remains so. Sushi purists may scoff at this. We ordered another round.

Three quivering, bronzed scallops—sweet with cinnamon, paired with sliced mango—are seared on the outside, quivering in the centre. With them, a single, perfect summer bean, a baby red pepper, a patty pan squash, a sprig of purple basil.

Braised baby bok choy and sautéed shiitake mushrooms fail to rescue the "golden crispy duck," which is indeed golden and crispy but also dry and tough. Dry and juiceless too are the strips of flank steak in a bowl of udon noodles, although the broth is complex and spicy. We are happiest with the Tsunami tuna, a fat chunk seared with mustard seeds, the flesh rare and luscious, served with grilled mushrooms and drizzled with a sauce that marries Cabernet with teriyaki.

The lemon tart is not quite set, but has magnificent flavour, dribbled with caramel and served with a ginger-flavoured tuile. A trio of crème brûlées—flavoured with lychee, passion fruit, and guava—are quite wonderful, as is a chocolate tart with a Mexican flair: flavoured with cinnamon and chillies, very dense, very smooth, very rich, very dark, served with a Chinese soupspoon of cinnamon ice cream.

There are many martinis here. There is a selection of sake and champagne by the half-bottle and full bottle. The wine list is small but varied, and almost every selection is available by the glass.

KINKI
41 York St. (between Sussex and Byward)
(613) 789-7559
www.kinki.ca
Access: Two steps into restaurant
Price: Main dishes $15 to $27
Open: Daily from noon to 1 A.M.

LA GAZELLE

★★ ½   **Moroccan** $

In Gatineau's only Moroccan restaurant you will find a traditional menu of tagines, brochettes, and couscous dishes. These are offered in a mustard-tinted room of ten tables spread with embroidered linen cloths. Some tables are surrounded with upholstered benches, some with dark wood chairs. The room is accented with Mediterranean colours—on pillows and curtains and in the traditional costume of the servers.

There are daily specials, particularly fine at lunch, when $9.95 will buy you a steaming bowl of the best harira soup in Hull (maybe even in the region), followed by a tagine served with couscous and a vibrant julienne of peppers, onion, carrot.

Dinner begins with carrots, rousing in a marinade of lemon, oil, garlic, cumin, and coriander. We order bestilla, a Moroccan party dish of shredded chicken (traditionally squab), almonds, onions, and egg wrapped in phyllo dough, baked and dusted with cinnamon and sugar. At our table are two fans and two foes of this sweet and savoury pie. I'm in the fan club, and I find La Gazelle's version moist, aromatic, and—once I'd blown off the bulk of the sugar dusting—just sweet enough. Others prefer the brik: deep-fried turnovers filled with shrimp and served with a well-flavoured tomato sauce.

There are tagines, each marked by a sensuous interplay of flavours. Some are sharp, cooked with preserved lemons, cumin, onions, olives, and artichokes. Some are sweet, like the lamb with prunes, honey, cinnamon, coriander, dried fruits, and nuts.

The brochettes we sample are grand in flavour, heady with coriander, but the meat suffers—as brochette meats tend to—from a certain aridness. They come with an abundance of steamed vegetables and couscous.

For dessert there is my kind of baklava—loads of nuts balanced with phyllo, not dripping in sugar syrup. And then spearmint tea, served with some ceremony from an ornate silver pot.

There is a collection of Moroccan reds to drink with this good food.

LA GAZELLE
33, rue Gamelin
Gatineau (Hull district)
(819) 777-3850
Access: Two steps into restaurant, tight foyer; washrooms are small; ramp to the summer patio is accessible
Price: Main dishes $12.95 to $14.95
Open: Lunch Tues.-Fri.; dinner Tues.-Sun.; closed Mon.

LAPOINTE
SEAFOOD GRILL

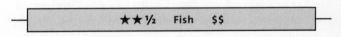

★★ ½   Fish $$

Is there anything more healing, after a cacophonous hour in a skateboard shop trying to fill a thirteen-year-old boy's Christmas wish list of "bearings" and "decks" and films entitled *Running with Scissors*, than a mug of workmanlike clam chowder? I tell you, there is not.

That soup was taken in the basement café of the Lapointe Fish Market. It was the most powerfully delicious thing I've tasted for ages. (Had I ordered it after, say, a day at the spa, it might have been only "very nice.")

You can buy Lapointe fish in six locations scattered around the region. At this Byward Market Lapointe's, the raw materials are displayed on the main floor. But down below, where a school of hand-painted fish swims around the sunny yellow room, you can have them boiled, steamed, shucked, battered, fried, grilled, spiced up, sauced over, or buck-naked. You can also have them raw, as the café has added a "menu Japonais" delivered by the new sushi bar upstairs.

In the summer, you can eat it all outside. In December, better to descend the stairs, where a cold tank of lobster and a warm fire greet you. A cheerful fellow will lead you over the tiled floor to one of thirty bare cherry wood tables set with paper napkins.

And so, the soup. Yes, it is a fine version, brimming with red skin-on potatoes, chunks of bacon, parsley, cream, and loads of clams. A mountain of calamari is tender and makes for thoroughly addictive munching. A five-shrimp starter is slightly over-grilled but drizzled with a yummy Mexican-inspired sauce, spiked with chillies and rounded with bitter chocolate; beside it, a small mound of sprightly greens.

The fish and chips are first-class: two thick hunks of battered halibut, judiciously fried to lacy crispness, served with long, superior French fries that are worth whatever dietary misery they cost. You can skip the rather grey, limp coleslaw in the ubiquitous metal cup. Better upgrade to the Caesar salad, which is as pungent as you'd hoped and topped with a generous grating of good Parmesan.

Dessert amounts to one fruit crumble, every crumb eaten.

LAPOINTE SEAFOOD GRILL

55 York St. (between Byward and William)
(613) 241-6221
Access: Phone ahead — access from parking garage through back door of restaurant; washrooms are small
Price: Main dishes $9 to $18
Open: Daily for lunch and dinner

LA TABLE DE PIERRE DELAHAYE

★★★   French $$$

In the wee town of Papineauville, about an hour's drive from Ottawa en route to Montebello and ski country, you'll find this nineteenth-century house. La Table de Pierre Delahaye is very much a hometown kind of place. It has a lacy, great-auntie's-tea-room feel to it. The sparkling crystal chandelier is on full-blast. The dozen tables are covered with pink cloths. Many framed awards are spread over the bright white walls, as are maps of France's wine-growing regions. And here and there—on the marble man-telpiece, hanging from a wee white tree, and featured throughout the menu—are red apples; a theme here.

This Table specializes in the cooking of the apple-rich region of Normandy, from whence cometh the chef. The setting may be a bit precious, but not the food. The flavours are true, the cooking is precise, and the dishes are no-nonsense, back-to-the-basics, through-and-through French classics.

There are two tables d'hôtes on offer. The first is an assembly of lighter dishes, bereft of the butter and cream we usually associate with Normandy cooking. The second is a more regional, seasonal list. À la carte is where you find the saucy stuff—the wine-boosted, cream-splashed, butter-mounted, satin-smooth sauces chef Pierre does so gloriously well.

You will do well to begin with soup. A cream of onion is long on onion flavour, rich with a good stock, and perfumed with a splash of framboise liqueur. A tiny dice of roasted apple perks up the cream of leek. Salads are pristine leaves of Boston lettuce (and only Boston lettuce), their buttery goodness dressed simply with a mustard-strong vinaigrette.

We ask if a main dish of ris de veau can be served as a starter portion. "Mais bien sûr, madame," is the reply from Madame Delahaye. The sweetbreads are delicate, milky-soft, braised with apples (bien sûr), napped with a slightly sweet cider and cream sauce. The apple theme continues to run throughout the meal: escargots are plump, garlicky, oozing butter, fragrant of the Normandy Calvados in which they are flambéed, spilling out of a flourish of browned phyllo.

The fish of the day is pickerel, perfumed with thyme, cooked gently, set in a well-flavoured sauce rich with cream and piquant with capers. Caribou is bright pink, tender, blood-juicy, its full-flavoured demi-glace sauce dotted with softened currants. Vegetables are seasonal and well done.

An apple tart with a thick layer of pastry cream ends the theme in a happy way. We scrape the plate. Madame Delahaye notices. "My husband is very good, oui?" she says with a smile in challenged, charming English.

Oui.

The wine list too is all-French.

LA TABLE DE PIERRE DELAHAYE
247 Papineau (off Hwy 148)
Papineauville
(819) 427-5027
Access: Three steps to entrance; washrooms are accessible
Price: Four-course table d'hôte $23.50 to $33.50
Open: Lunch Wed.-Fri. and Sun.; dinner Wed.-Sat.; closed Mon. and Tues.

LAURIER SUR MONTCALM

★★★★   **French** $$$$

"Ohhh, honey," he bleated. "I'm not up for a fancy French restaurant tonight. Couldn't we just do a simple place?"

By "simple" he means a quick-paced, order-eat-pay-go-home sort of place. Dining to be endured before the reward of sleep.

After ten years of heavy-duty eating-out, my husband still doesn't get it. The chore in one of his so-called "simple" eateries is usually spending your evening trying to catch the waiter's eye to get a glass of water, or a fresh fork, or some explanation of what you're about to eat.

By contrast, the glorious, effortless ease with which a Laurier sur Montcalm dinner unfolds is as soothing to the bushed senses as a Bing Crosby lullaby. It is a gently paced series of exquisite mouthfuls, not meant to startle with assaulting combinations so much as to lull you with its symphonic ingredients, brilliantly assembled by the hands of Chef Georges Laurier.

And such service. You mention you're a bit chilly, and an angora wrap is produced; you ask about a glass of wine to match the ris de veau, and your server knows just the one. The total familiarity with the food, the wines, and the matching thereof is admirable. No effort is involved on the part of the diner. And you leave feeling refreshed. It's just that simple.

And they have French champagne by the glass. How simply wonderful is that?

An amuse-bouche of sushi tuna is finely diced, moistened with a chervil-scented oil, and paired with organic pink beets. From there, a seductive soup of roasted butternut squash, unadulterated but for the pretty swirl of intense beet purée.

And then a starter of lamb confit. It is glorious, mellow meat, de-fatted but of intensely rich flavour, united with strands of caramel-ized red onion, sharpened with mustard enfolded in a pasta pouch, and set in a deep pool of densely lamby jus.

The fish cake is so powerfully sea-rich that you can almost taste the shells. Bound with potato, browned, roasted, set on a "röstis" of grated carrot, it is moistened with a clean, light, lemony sauce. Paper-thin lemon slices, dipped in the lightest tempura batter and deep-fried for a second, are the two airy bursts of intense flavour that are the icing on this cake.

The ris de veau are soft nuggets, livened with an intense veal sauce piqued with reduced balsamic vinegar. A breast of duck is utterly straightforward, moist inside with a thin layer of fat for flavour, and a bronzed, leaf-thin crispy skin holding it all together. Wild rice studded with almonds and raisins, and a mélange of root vegetables—parsnips, turnip, carrot—completes the plate.

A faultless crème brûlée infused with espresso and an apple tarte with Calvados-infused crème anglaise arrives for dessert. Truffles come with coffee. Simply magnificent.

LAURIER SUR MONTCALM

199, rue Montcalm (between Taché and St. Joseph)
Gatineau (Hull district)
(819) 775-5030
www.lauriersurmontcalm.com
Access: Fully accessible
Price: Main dishes $21 to $41; three-course table d'hôte
$31 to $47
Open: Lunch Tues.-Fri.; dinner Tues.-Sat.; closed Sun. and Mon.

LE BACCARA

★★★★   French $$$$

After hours of gracious, seamless service and many plates of deeply pleasurable food over the course of two Baccara dinners, in some perverse effort to find fault, I flagged the young woman in charge of the water, bread, and coffee service. I asked her a question about the disk thing that came with my lobster. (Of course, she wouldn't have a clue . . . she's the water girl.)

"It is an oatmeal galette, madame. Is it to your liking?" She bestowed a sweet, shy smile and topped up my water glass (natural spring, of course).

These people know their jobs. They exemplify teamwork. When they aren't tending tables, they're standing on guard. When you leave for the loo, a fresh napkin welcomes you back. And they know the food, every nuance of it, inside out and upside down. All of them.

You pay the price, of course, for this level of service, for this food, for a wine cellar that offers a mess of premier cru, but so be it. You will not find much better in this city. Dust off your dinner jacket (you'll need one, gentlemen), pay off the Visa, invent an occasion, and come.

The menu is long: eleven starters, three soups, and ten main dishes on the menu du saison. There's the menu gourmand, the menu dégustation, the menu gastronomique (both with "palettes de vin"), and finally, the menu dégustation végétarien. And then there's the heavy carte de vin. It's a good read, and a long one.

Chef Serge Rourre's cooking is firmly anchored in first-rate ingredients and solid French traditions. His work is imaginative — exotic, even — but always grounded in culinary common sense.

That oatmeal galette was paired with seafood—an arrangement of supple, just-seared scallops and sweet-fleshed langoustine, moistened with an oceanic butter sauce, and crowned with shredded leeks. Paper-thin slices of smoked lamb arrived with baked goat cheese, surrounded with oil-slicked oyster mushrooms and a fruity-sweet, peppery-sharp chutney. And then tuna, seared and rare, shared a plate with tempura-dressed, nori-wrapped salmon and a rich purée of halibut with oil and garlic. Sensational.

The soupe de coquillages was ladled into its warmed bowl table-side, over a mound of waiting seafood threaded with strands of sweet leek and carrot, accented with minced chives and feathery dill. I didn't look up until it was gone.

Meltingly good foie gras, seared on the outside, soft and pliant within, came surrounded by a piece of perfect snapper, its softness offset with a mound of creamy, crackling quinoa. Fresh chanterelle mushrooms, lentils, and an anise-scented chutney of apples and red onion were the striking accents of a plate of boar chops, roasted to rare and moistened with a polished sauce of vibrant gamey flavour.

You must include in Le Baccara's assets sommelière Danielle Dupont, a tiny woman of considerable charm who's seemingly acquainted personally with each of the 16,000 wine bottles she manages.

A round of local chèvre from the cheese trolley, and then a plate of exquisite mignardises from the pastry chef. Brilliant.

LE BACCARA
1, boul. du Casino (at Casino du Lac Leamy)
Gatineau (Hull district)
(819) 772-6210
www.casinodulacleamy.com
Access: Fully accessible
Price: Main dishes $29 to $49; menu dégustation $69; menu gastronomique $115
Open: Daily for dinner only
Dress code applies

LE CAFÉ

★ ★ ½   **Canadian – Contemporary** $$$

On chef Kurt Waldele's stage beneath the National Arts Centre, the performance is impressive.

One evening we are in Le Café's main room, elegant in white with deep blue accents, photographs of performers on every column, mini lights prettying the November view of the canal. Another visit, we're in the seating area just above the dining room, used for overflow. Both nights we are well fed, though not without some wrong notes — but for the most part, a superior show.

The seafood chowder is a winner — always has been — with its fresh clams and soft salmon in a full-flavoured bisque. The house Caesar has all the proper elements of success. The tuna tartare is glorious. It gets its zip from a side of pickled ginger and another of chopped red onions. The plate is finished with a soft-boiled quail egg, a spear of pappadum, and a forgettable piece of sushi — cold rice around a boiled carrot. The goat-cheese flavour is weak in a tart rimmed with too-thick, tired-tasting pastry. It's the one let-down among the starters.

When it comes to main dishes, the choices are solid, reliable; not feats of gastronomy, but very agreeable indeed. The rack of lamb is excellent. It arrives rare, as ordered, with a satisfying treatment of mint, mustard, and garlic roasted into its surfaces. The other joy of this dish is the accompanying mound of crusty, oil-soused potatoes layered with a black olive tapenade. Yellow cloudberries from Newfoundland are fashioned into a relish and provide a sweet-tart foil for the rare, thick steak of venison. The meat is lean, gamey-flavoured, and succulent, served with good mashed potatoes, grated turnip and — what's this? — asparagus.

For a kitchen that celebrates Canadian cuisine, it seems wrong to offer these May shoots in November. They are, not surprisingly, tasteless.

The weak main dish we encounter is the Brome Lake duck. We like the candied lemon in the polished sauce of blood orange and duck jus, but despite its bronzed surface, the meat within tastes stewed.

For dessert, a velvety crème brûlée, a delicious apple tart, and luscious sorbet.

These dishes are in the company of a wine list strong on Canadian content, with good choices by the glass, and most bottles in the $30 to $40 range.

For those in a pre-performance hurry, or who just don't want to spend time mulling over the menu, there is an express table d'hôte: soup or salad, chicken, salmon, or beef.

LE CAFÉ
National Arts Centre
53, Elgin St. (at Laurier)
(613) 594-5127
www.nac-can.ca
Access: Fully accessible
Price: Main dishes $19.95 to $33.95; table d'hôte $24.95 to $29.95 (after 8 P.M., table d'hôte is $19.95)
Open: Lunch and dinner Mon.-Fri.; dinner only Sat.

L'ÉCHELLE DE JACOB

★★   French $$$

I was a fan of Café Wisigoth, a modest, mostly-mussels restaurant on Beechwood Avenue that was forced to close about five years ago. The husband-and-wife team that was Wisigoth has since bought L'Échelle de Jacob, an established restaurant on Lucerne Boulevard in what was formely Aylmer (now Gatineau).

The place is well hidden. A small sign on the side of the busy boulevard helps; but even when you discover the turnoff, you need to search this century-old grey building—once a mill, then a streetcar depot, now apartments—to find a second sign that directs you into a cloudy, sky-blue stairwell and up to the second level.

There's a Québécois-tavern feel to Jacob, with its thick stone walls, dark wooden beams, and black iron chandeliers. The tables are laid with white cloths. Candles spread throughout the room further the rustic-romantic atmosphere.

Curiously, there are no mussels on the one-page spring menu. (Perhaps chef Marianne is weary of them.) Begin instead with the goat cheese starter, a light, beautifully seasoned soufflé with luscious Floralpe Farms cheese rising out of the mould. Or try the scallops, chopped and treated with lime juice, then wrapped in succulent slices of smoked salmon. The bundles are balanced with a mustard sauce sweetened with honey, a simple application that stands up to the rich salmon and balances the sour-acidity of the scallops.

And there are more successful first courses: mushrooms, some wild, some tame, are layered with bread charlotte-style and bathed in a rich cream sauce of good woodsy flavour. A ripe, rustic gaz-pacho has a pleasant, spicy bite, and a Moroccan chorba is an aromatic broth thick with legumes and lamb.

The best of the mains is the quail—the wee legs are plump and moist, and we like the side of fresh couscous steamed with a dash of curry and filled out with raisins and almonds—but the breast meat is on the dry side. The salmon is fresh but overcooked; and the handsome grill marks that crisscross the beef fillet look appe-tizing, but a burnt flavour has permeated the meat.

Back to form with dessert: full marks for the fabulous profiteroles, the choux puffs just-baked fresh, the sauce dark and luscious, and for the lime cheesecake: full fat, full flavour, fully enjoyed.

L'ÉCHELLE DE JACOB
27, boul. Lucerne (at chemin Vanier)
Gatineau (Aylmer district)
(819) 684-1040
Access: Restaurant is on the second level
Price: Table d'hôte $30 to $36
Open: Dinner only Wed.-Sun.

LE JARDIN

★★ ½   French $$$$

Le Jardin is an *ancien régime* restaurant that has survived, seemingly unaffected by the whims of any culinary trend du jour, for close to thirty years. What this York Street restaurant does right is offer The Big Night Out: largely familiar French dishes complemented by an admirable French wine list, served by a properly trained staff in the setting of a gracious heritage home.

For a great many people, there is comfort in a menu weighted in tradition, wrapped in leather, free of anxiety-inducing ingredients, and listing the full complement of recognizable classics — such standards as escargots, consommé, foie gras, sweetbreads, rack of lamb, chocolate marquise.

Over the course of two dinners here, we encountered a perfectly executed seafood velouté with an intense broth and excellent fish (scallops, shrimp, lobster), as well as a properly made, well-seasoned poultry consommé. We've had a first-class pâté de chevreuil, rimmed with fat (comme il faut), moist, meaty, perfumed with fresh thyme, studded with hazelnuts and served with a sweet thyme jelly. And we've had plump, garlicky snails in a fine puff pastry, buoyed up by a lively tomato sauce.

We've also enjoyed a presentation of smoked scallops and salmon, but with it came a "lemongrass" mousseline that had no discernible lemongrass flavour. We've struggled with a wild mushroom soup of very tame mushroom flavour, a lobster salad dressed with an unpleasantly sweet cassis vinaigrette, and a starter of tough shrimp in a curiously tasteless papaya coulis. And surely I could have ripe mango (as opposed to the rock-hard slices I was served) with my $23.95 starter of a less-than-generous morsel of seared foie gras.

But the medaillon de veau was worth every penny of its price tag: two thick slabs of succulent veal, pungent with grill flavours, and napped with a robust peppercorn sauce. The salmon was soft, the beurre blanc supporting it perfect, and the beef tenderloin faultless. But then a letdown in a breast of duck, cooked to medium-rare but tough as boots, napped with a kumquat and lime sauce that did nothing for me. Nothing not to like about the seasonal vegetables, though: fiddleheads, asparagus, tarragon-glazed carrots, and young potatoes with a good béarnaise sauce completed the dinner plates.

For dessert, a chocolate terrine of exceptional chocolate flavour, and a yummy French cheesecake glazed with apricot and surrounded with fresh berries.

The long wine list is mainly French and mainly expensive, but then this is the kind of setting where splurging is encouraged. We, for example, were directed to a $265 magnum. We declined.

LE JARDIN
127 York St. (between Cumberland and Dalhousie)
(613) 241-1424
www.lejardin.biz
Access: One step into restaurant; washrooms are on second floor
Price: Main dishes $18.95 to $32.95
Open: Daily for dinner only

LE PANACHÉ

★★★   French $$$

The trick to enjoying Le Panaché is to focus on the food.

The small L-shaped room is not without some poky charm. But it is weary-looking. The floors are white ceramic in places, salmon-coloured in others; the walls are divided between pine-panelled bottoms and terracotta-coloured tops. There's a cluttered feeling to the Sante Fe–style, New Age–ish knickknacks.

In contrast to the casual look, the service is polished. But my bet is that it's the precise, inspired cooking that keeps the Panaché chairs filled.

Top-notch bread starts things off. At dinner, a potato soup is livened up with a hit of lemon, meaty with bacon. At lunch, a fresh tomato soup has summer tomato depth and an exotic splash of coconut milk. Le Panaché's salads are inspired creations of generous portion. A towering beauty of many tender greens, speared with endive and fried carrot strings, is dressed with eggs, red peppers, ripe mango, and capers in a mustard-balsamic vinaigrette. Many might have made a meal of it, but we soldiered on with perfect mussels in a lemongrass-enhanced broth littered with black beans and leeks. The last of our bread soaked up the last of the sauce. However, underdone edges of pasta slightly marred the otherwise successful seafood-stuffed ravioli in a Pernod and dill cream sauce.

Main dishes at dinner include a perfectly executed rack of lamb and a faultless beef fillet. The former is classically smeared with rosemary, garlic, and mustard, and the rare beef with caramelized shallots is served in a rich, port-spiked demi-glace. A plate of quail is totally successful: three wee ones boned and served with two puddles of sauce, a banana curry and a honey-sweetened demi-glace. The one letdown is a dried-out roast of caribou. We made a meal of the vegetables instead—baby bok choy, caramelized onions, grilled pineapple, zucchini, carrots, turnip, and red cabbage.

Wine suggestions (available by the glass) are listed with the main dishes, a user-friendly practice I root for.

Cheers too for the desserts: for the fabulous chocolate sauce on the "decadent" crêpe, for the beautifully ripe pineapple, grilled and served with ice cream and caramel sauce, and for the impeccable crème brûlée.

And finally, for the service.

LE PANACHÉ
201, rue Eddy (at St. Laurent)
Gatineau (Hull district)
(819) 777-7771
Access: One step at entrance; washrooms are accessible
Price: Main dishes $18.95 to $24.95
Open: Lunch Tues.-Fri.; daily for dinner

LE PIED DE COCHON

★★   French $$$

Le Pied de Cochon has had the same chef, same owner for all of its twenty-eight years. It presents a no-nonsense line-up of French bistro classics; and when I weary, as I sometimes do, of long, riddling menus and labyrinthine dish descriptions, I find this menu a comfort. "Langoustines façon provençale," "filet de boeuf au poivre," "gratin de fruits de mer." There is even the classic médaillon de veau "à ma façon"—leaving you with the impression that you'll get your veal according to the chef's whim du moment. A dish description on this menu involves, on average, five words—all in French. I have never seen an English version.

Service is neither overbearing nor overly familiar. When you need the wait staff, they are there. Otherwise, they are scarce and detached. The front of the house is run by a stern figure. He knows his business well enough, but bestowing a welcoming grin is just not his thing. Perhaps if you're one of the folk who come here regularly, your reception is warmer. I can speak only of my own experience.

There are two rooms. Both are fairly large; one is better looking, with more character. The other is cluttered with competing colours.

Focus on the steak tartare. There are few restaurants in this region that do it well, and this is one of them. The dish is a plate of hand-minced raw beef, the red meat enriched with capers, onion, pickles, and a touch of cayenne, the flavours well balanced and the whole effect very pleasing.

But as reliable as the tartare is, dinner at Le Pied de Cochon can be an uneven affair. The lobster bisque tastes as though it began well but was watered down; the full seafood quality doesn't reach you. The mussels are many but overcooked. The terrine, however, is full-flavoured and nicely textured, and the duck confit is a great success—the skin bronzed, the flesh tender, the leg set in a salad of frisée and radicchio, lightly dressed.

Duck again, as a main, is correctly cooked to medium-rare, set in a honey-sweetened sauce perfumed with framboise. The fish of the evening is lotte (monkfish), buttery-soft, beautifully cooked—but with it come chunks of mushy lobster.

At lunch, the rouleau de printemps is little more than lettuce, baby shrimp, and overcooked vermicelli wrapped in softened rice paper. It has no sparkle, no flavour. Better to order the gazpacho, which is a pleasant bowl of summer's bounty. The noon entrecôte is as you order it, medium-rare, handsomely crosshatched by the grill, thin but juicy, garnished with a béarnaise sauce that's buttery enough, but not particularly sharp or fragrant. Frites come alongside; they are thin and of good potato flavour.

The "profiteroles" are merely stale choux puffs filled with supermarket Neapolitan ice cream, topped with a weak chocolate sauce.

Next time, I may just order another round of raw steak for dessert.

LE PIED DE COCHON
242, rue Montcalm
Gatineau (Hull district)
(819) 777-5808
Access: One step into restaurant; washrooms are down three steps
Prices: Main dishes $18.50 to $28.50
Open: Lunch Tues.-Fri.; dinner Tues.-Sat.; closed Sun. and Mon.

LE SAINT O

★★★   French $$$

One of the great perks of this job used to be the fairly frequent, all-expenses-paid dinner dates with my husband, during which he would chatter charmingly and gaze lovingly while I ate his food and made notes. Truly our salad days—post-kids, yes, but pre-school.

These days, I dine out more and more often with others; and his evenings happen at home amid the heady contents of school knapsacks. These are the homework days.

Still, I save Le Saint O for our rare dates. You can hardly take any old friend to eat garlic-soused escargots, or milky-sweet sea scallops coddled on a crackling cradle of deep-fried potato, napped with a seductive beurre blanc, and finished with glistening salmon roe.

Le Saint O is just that kind of place: an enduring French restaurant on St. Laurent Boulevard, surrounded by nothing much but field behind, cemetery ahead, and mini-malls around. It caters mostly to the Manor Park-Rockcliffe-New Edinburgh-Lindenlea neighbourhoods to the west, and to those farther afield who are prepared to go the distance for the sake of its food.

On inspection from busy St. Laurent, Le Saint O is a largely unremarkable little white house—prettiest in the patio days, when its front arbours are covered in green vine. Inside, though, is an elegant room neatly divided into intimate seating areas, the tables impeccably set, the chairs designed to fit you well. You are warmly greeted and well served by owner Natasha Dumont, and you will be very well fed by chef Philippe Dupuy. His menu is rife with French classics sporting Québécois accents: ris de veau with local honey, duck confit with maple syrup, lamb rack with mustard sauce, beef fillet with Roquefort butter. His soups and sauces are rich with flavour; his cooking of game inspired; his desserts delicious.

Two signature dishes are always on form: duos, or sometimes trios, of soup, in which vegetable purées are poured simultaneously into one bowl, each colour, each flavour separate, yet together — a purée of carrot on the left, perhaps, and broccoli on the right, or a third purée of beet scented with orange in its own corner. Grated apple, toasted pine nuts or caramelized onion garnish the top. Whatever the inspiration, the purées sing out with flavour. And then there are the house sweetbreads, seared and soft, treated with vermouth, honey, and cream, always on this menu and always worth ordering.

Lightly smoked salmon, pale and moist, is layered with ripe mango and avocado, the pretty construct dobbed and dribbled with a fruity plum-and-red-currant sauce.

Pork tenderloin is crusted with sun-dried tomatoes, the salty, pungent flavours marrying well and the meat quite perfectly pale pink and moist. Salmon is crisp-skinned outside and effortless inside, napped with a polished beurre blanc, lively with lemon, and anchored with lotus root. Garlicky mashed potatoes, butternut squash, and local asparagus round out these plates.

Dessert is a luscious nut torte, layered and lightened with a proper butter cream.

Le Saint O's wine list is all-French, offering both ordinary and extraordinary bottles.

LE SAINT O
327, boul. St. Laurent (at Hemlock)
(613) 749-9703
www.lesainto.com
Access: Five steps into restaurant; washrooms are small
Price: Three-course table d'hôte $32
Open: Lunch Tues.-Fri.; dinner Tues.-Sun.; closed Mon.

LE SANS PAREIL

★★★   French – Belgian $$$$

Ordering is an earnest task. It requires a thorough thinking-through. One must work out what is the best, the most appropriate, the most outré or tricky or signature dishes to taste. It is the most bothersome part of reviewing a restaurant. And it is likely the reason my husband has issues with my job.

"I think I feel like lamb tonight, Anne."

"No, you don't, darling. I think you feel like fish." And so it goes: all fun and chitchat shut down until the wretched business is concluded. A long menu just adds to the misery.

So what joy when one gets the chance to set aside the menu and just say, "Bring it on."

At Le Sans Pareil, a Belgian restaurant in Gatineau, the regular four-course table d'hôte is complemented with a "menu surprise": four courses of who-knows-what, accompanied by wines to match. And in chef/owner Luc Gielen's restaurant, the surprises are deeply pleasurable.

Dark caramel walls with wide white borders and dark cherry floors frame the two small dining rooms of Le Sans Pareil. The lighting is warm, the atmosphere comfortable, the ten or so tables formally set and graciously served by a couple of good guys.

"I think it's sweet," one dinner date once remarked, looking around the room, "How many books they've set aside for children here. I'm just not sure it's the sort of restaurant I'd take my kids to." Just then, menus arrived: *Tintin en Amérique* for her, *Les Bijoux du Castifiore* for me. The menus are clipped inside—a truly adult listing contained in a collection of Hergé comics.

Dinner begins with an amuse-gueule: a lamb rillette, the rendered fat adding flavour, the texture properly coarse. One soup is a delicate cream of vegetable, in which the cream provides only the smoothness, and the vegetables all the fragrance and flavour. The other is a dark roasted onion, further sweetened with patterns of caramelized balsamic.

The "surprise" starter is Brie de Meaux, the fragrant cheese wrapped and baked in phyllo, bronzed and oozing, moistened with walnut oil, dotted with roasted walnuts, and served with a delightful apple compote. And then a buttery sauté of wild mushrooms and lardons, treated with a warm dousing of balsamic, set on a bed of wilted baby greens, the whole wrapped in long, thin strips of blanched cucumber. Venison is next, served pink, the flesh yielding, the flavour excellent, the red wine sauce impeccable.

There are veal kidneys on this menu, buried in flaky puff pastry, boosted by a dark sauce piqued with mustard. And there are mussels, of course, served in Belgian fashion with fabulous frites and a pot of eggy mayonnaise. The one disappointment is a risotto starter, in which garlicky escargots come off better than the gummy rice in which they are set.

The standout dessert is a warm Belgian chocolate pudding cake, with poached pears and a mascarpone cream.

The wine list is all-French.

LE SANS PAREIL
71, boul. St. Raymond
Gatineau (Hull district)
(819) 771-1471
Access: Fully accessible
Price: Table d'hôte $33 to $48
Open: Lunch Mon.-Fri.; dinner Mon.-Sat.; closed Sun.

LES FOUGÈRES

★★★★   **Canadian**   **$$$$**

A wall full of Epicurean awards, another of enthusiastic reviews, and now four new walls. These latest surround a store, complete with open kitchen, selling caribou-cranberry tourtière, wild mushroom soup, and bottles of Les Fougères' blackberry vinegar syrup.

All this speaks of the ten-year-old restaurant's commercial success and critical recognition.

But browsing through the guest books on the foyer table, it's "Beverly" who best sums up my feelings about Les Fougères. Her entry from 1998: "I love this place a lot. It rules. It rocks."

Indeed.

Les Fougères is a white house with a wide porch, dominated by pale pine and big windows, surrounded with tall trees. In summer you may sit outside on that porch. I always seem to visit in winter, when the backyard is filled with bird feeders and the fir trees are pretty with white lights.

The food, by chefs/owners Charles Part and Jennifer Warren-Part, is grounded in solid technique and solid flavours. They make creative use of top-quality seasonal ingredients, most of them plucked regionally. The service is kind and knowledgeable—but not so very formal, in keeping with the rustic setting.

For starters, there's a splendid plate of spring. Three juicy shrimp, grill-marked and grill-flavoured, are nestled on pasta moistened with chicken stock, plumped with soft, sweet onions, fresh peas, chunks of pancetta. A fat morsel of smoked char is parked in the centre of a bowl of potato soup, its mild, creamy flavour piqued with fresh horseradish and grainy mustard. Gentle swirls of mascarpone cheese provide a final flourish. The house ravioli is swooningly good. Filled with leek, spinach, Brie, and lightly cooked egg, and topped with a sweet-tart confit of red onion, it's set in an unctuous broth of wild mushrooms, enhanced with truffle oil, and further enriched by the escaping cheese and oozing egg. Yum.

For main courses, there are melt-in-the-mouth scallops teamed up with salt cod, perfectly milked of its saltiness. All is supported by braised celery root and a purée of potatoes, thinned with stock, shiny with olive oil.

And then a fusion success: a Flintstone-sized portion of succulent lamb is drenched with Indian spices, dotted with currants and bronzed cashews. A flourish of tempura-battered wisps of spinach and aromatic orange rind shares the plate.

Pickerel is the featured fish at a Fougères lunch. The fresh white fillet is paired with tart sections of pink grapefruit, set on a sweet purée of roasted parsnips, enhanced with an elegant sauce rich with caramelized onion and fragrant with rosemary. A hint of maple syrup sweetens the duck tourtière, thickened with a bit of potato, boosted with orange rind, baked in a buttery-rich pastry and served with a mustard-seed pickle and a zippy tomato-onion relish.

For dessert, a deep chocolate tart with a dark chocolate crust, a raspberry coulis and a blueberry compote: one slice, three forks, three purring women.

Les Fougères has received a Wine Spectator award for its list.

So was there a problem anywhere? Yes: the salad that came with the tourtière was overdressed. There.

It still rocks, though.

LES FOUGÈRES
783, Route 105 (at Scott)
Chelsea
(819) 827-8942
www.fougeres.com
Access: Steps up to front door, more into restaurant
Price: Main dishes $21.50 to $32; table d'hôte $39
Open: Daily for lunch and dinner

LE TARTUFFE

★★★ ½   French $$$

No truffles, no caviar, no alarming prices, no confusing pairings of complicated ingredients: just the principles of modern French cuisine applied to fresh regional produce, and the expertise to pull off consistently excellent eating. It's hardly news that Le Tartuffe is a very good French restaurant. What's noteworthy is that it has remained a very good French restaurant for a long time now.

You make a slow and happy progress through chef/owner Gérard Fischer's table d'hôte. In September, it may begin with gazpacho, an intensely fruity and dill-scented bowl of fall's bounty. There is duck next, some of it fresh and some of it smoked, all of it carefully hand-chopped, molded into neat quenelle-shaped nuggets and served with a salad of grated celery root.

A second soup is a perfectly seasoned, deeply pleasurable bowl of leek. A whole pear arrives scarlet from its poaching in mulled wine, stuffed with local goat cheese and flavoured with a drizzle of pistachio oil.

Sauces are brilliant here. A sharp, buttery liquid of roast drippings spiked with red wine and grainy mustard naps a properly meaty, cranberry-stuffed roasted quail. The intensely boozy, thyme-scented liquid in which the morels are plumped adds flavour to the sweet, woodsy sauce that anoints a moist breast of pheasant, heady with its stuffing of wild boar and wild mushroom. This comes with spaghetti squash, snow peas, a wedge of gratin dauphinois (potatoes sliced and baked with cheese and garlic) and a mound of ratatouille laden with yellow and green zucchini.

An early fall lunch on Le Tartuffe's pretty deck begins with a saffron-coloured seafood chowder with white fish, shrimp, and salmon, the broth light yet rich with seafood flavour. And then pork medaillons, slightly pink, smeared and seared with mustard and thyme, a drizzle of honey in the sauce. One letdown is a somewhat overgrilled salmon, though it is moistened nicely with a very fine fennel-flavoured beurre blanc.

Despite my resolve to order desserts other than the crème brûlée — which I already know to be superb — I cave: we tuck in to one thrilling-as-ever crème brûlée and one mango cheesecake, smooth, rich, and with clear mango flavour.

Le Tartuffe's waiters know their job: they are knowledgeable and their technique is sound, but they do not dote. If you want your dinner to speed along, best to let them know. You are expected to linger at Le Tartuffe, each delicious course delivered at a leisurely pace.

LE TARTUFFE

133, rue Notre-Dame de l'Île (at Papineau)
Gatineau (Hull district)
(819) 776-6424
www.letartuffe.com
Access: Fully accessible
Price: Table d'hôte from $28 to $36
Open: Lunch Mon.-Fri.; dinner Mon.-Sat.; closed Sun.

LE VERLAN

★ ★ ★ ½   French $$$

"Very good, madame. I look forward to seeing you at seven, then. Your table will be waiting for you."

Classy, eh? And surely not so very difficult. (Although by virtue of its noteworthiness, you'd think it nearly impossible.)

A superior telephone greeting tells me that someone is pleased I'm coming; someone is going to be looking out for me. My table will be ready, the candles will be lit, the wine glasses polished, and my coat will likely not be relegated to the back of my chair.

Combine that hospitality with a first-class kitchen, add a thoughtful wine list, a staff trained to guide me through it, a few good friends, and it doesn't much matter whether I'm sitting in a posh and pricy designer space (not the case) or a rec room (you're getting warmer). Either way, I've got all I need to feel like a million bucks.

Which is exactly how Le Verlan makes me feel.

The walls have been redone since my last visit, the lighting updated, and some (but not all) of the kitschier knickknacks removed. But Le Verlan remains a small, cosy, largely unremarkable space. Plainness notwithstanding, the food is delicious, served with obvious pride; a balance of elegant pretension and joie de vivre that is somehow—and hugely—refreshing.

Much of the joie comes from the chef and co-owner, Daniel Verlati, who power-walks about the room in his whites, talking wine, talking food, taking orders, busing tables, and laughing, laughing, laughing. On the merits of a particular wine: "I bring you the bottle, if you don't like, no problem—I'll drink it later." On why he isn't in the kitchen: "I cooked all day, now the dishwasher is finishing for me." On the sweetbreads: "Go right there." On the foie gras: "Don't think about the money, think about the taste."

He is clearly delighted with himself. We are delighted with his food.

He starts us off with a superior smoked fish pâté set simply on toast. Then two soups: squash and apple with ginger, and carrot and orange with coriander—both bowls pure, fragrant, perfect.

As advised, I damn the price and head straight for the foie gras: seared, all quivering succulence inside, adorned with roasted, caramelized apples, presented on a grilled oiled baguette, and set in a woodsy, bittersweet sauce mounted with port and bittersweet dark chocolate. It is a striking plate of food.

Plump escargots have a voluptuous texture, set on a thin round of perfect pasta, in a buttery-rich sauce thick with wild mushrooms and their juices. The soufflé of goat cheese is light but rich in good chèvre flavour, perfumed by its basil-breadcrumb crust, and rimmed with a tomato coulis lightly fired with chillies. And a final starter of sushi, Le Verlan–style, which brings together luscious house-smoked salmon and perfect sea scallops with vinegared rice, daikon, nori, seaweed, chervil, and salmon roe, in an enormously appealing way.

Next round of hits: tuna, its glistening red interior in dramatic contrast to the charred edges, topped with a beurre blanc; hefty slices of gamey pork, lean but remarkably moist, stuffed with celery, sage, apples, and with blueberries stirred into its dark sauce. And more: medaillons of caribou, beautifully marked by the grill, this sauce also finished with chocolate; and beef tenderloin, lightly smoked before being fired, the flavour quite subtle but very there, the meat sliced and rimmed with rounds of Jerusalem artichoke and quenelle-shaped mounds of mashed potato, perfumed with sage and white chocolate.

Chocolate in the sauce, chocolate in the spuds , who needs dessert?

Apparently, we do. A pear and almond tart, a strawberry mousse piped with grilled meringue and served with strawberry sorbet; a fabulous crème brûlée flavoured with maple syrup, the custard light, smooth, its caramelized top warm, thin, crackling. And just in case, something chocolate. Three treatments: a mousse, a fondant, a terrine — all desserts completed with constructions of spun sugar.

A plate of mignardises arrives. We rise to the challenge. The tea is loose-leaf, the coffee fresh and strong, delivered with a variety of sugars, none in packets, and pots of real milk and real cream.

Which seems right. Le Verlan is the real thing. Your coats will be delivered to you, the door will be held open as you leave. Do you really need more reason to return?

LE VERLAN
222, rue Laval (at Sacré Cœur)
Gatineau (Hull district)
(819) 777-8883
Access: Wheelchair access into restaurant; washrooms are small
Price: Five-course table d'hôte $29.95
Open: Dinner only Tues.-Sat.

LITTLE INDIA CAFÉ

★★   Indian $

Well, it's still little. That hasn't changed. And it remains a very simple place, found in a strip mall directly across from the Coliseum movieplex. What's new is the menu: the Little India Café has gone north. It now offers what pretty much every other restaurant in the region offers, namely the food of Northern India, Punjabi-style. With the exception of Sunday brunch, the Little India Café no longer serves what the menu once described as the cooking of the "mystic south."

So I missed my idli with coconut sauce; and the masala dosa I was expecting to find (a tablecloth-sized rice "crêpe" stuffed with spiced potatoes) was nowhere on this new menu. But what a grand butter chicken they gave me, and what a richness and complexity of spicing in the lamb bhuna. And thankfully unchanged were the vegetarian dishes, which continue to be among this kitchen's strengths.

Good too are the Little India soups. A brown bowl of the Anglo-Indian mulligatawny was brimming with moist chicken and lentils, its broth assertive with cumin, mustard seeds, and curry leaves, tart with lemon, spicy with chillies, enriched lightly with coconut milk. The tandoori chicken was perfectly tender and juicy beneath its charred pink skin, its flavour smoky and pungent from its tandoor roasting and the spices and yogurt of its marinade. It arrived on a platter with a colourful tangle of onion and peppers.

We fought over the shrimp, for there were not many in the Kashmiri-style curry. But they were large and good, swimming in a cashew-studded sauce rich with cream, tangy with yogurt, and just right for naan dunking. Chunks of salmon were coated with a ginger-potent sauce plump with tomatoes and onions, scented with coriander and cardamom. The spiciest dish, in terms of the chilli heat, was the lamb bhuna: fork-tender chunks of lamb with soft onions and crisp peppers in a sauce deep with flavour, splendid with freshly ground roasted spices.

Vegetarian dishes we sampled were all hits: sag paneer (spinach and homemade cheese); aloo gobi masala (a curry of potatoes, cauliflower and tomatoes); and, always my favourite, the baigan bharta: eggplant, roasted whole and cooked with tomatoes and onion — fabulous for its smokiness, its pungency, its flavour.

To cool the palate, there was raita; and to fire it up, the Parsi-style onion salad called kachumbar, with chunks of tomato, cucumber, and onion spiked with fresh coriander, ginger, and chillies.

Service was attentive and personal throughout.

LITTLE INDIA CAFÉ
66, Wylie Ave. (at Carling)
(613) 828-2696
Access: No steps, but restaurant, including washrooms, is very small — call ahead
Price: Main dishes $7.95 to $14.95
Open: Lunch Sun.-Fri.; dinner daily

LITTLE TURKISH VILLAGE

★★   Turkish $

After many years of business, the Little Turkish Village continues to thrive in Orléans, with the same owners, the same menu, and the same remarkably good value for the dining-out dollar. The ingredients are right, the portions are generous, and the dishes are freshly made. It isn't food worth crossing town for, but Willie Chan (yes, that's right, Chan) doesn't appear to need customers from anywhere else. Orléans keeps him plenty busy.

For newcomers to Turkish food, it's a lot like the more familiar Greek food—and with good reason. Many foods can be easily traced to their Greek origins (and vice versa), and many Turkish dishes have Greek names.

The "special meze salad," for $5, feeds three of us easily. Dolma are spinach-stained rice and currants wrapped in grape leaves. The rice tastes fresh; the packages are fragrant. There's a dollop of Patlican salad (not unlike the Greek melitzano salata) of mashed roasted eggplant, seasoned liberally with onion, tomato, parsley, garlic, and lemon juice; and another dollop of hummus, strong of garlic, lemon, reddened with paprika. And still more: a mound of Turkish potato salad called ankara, and spinach borek: phyllo-wrapped, spinach-feta stuffed pastries. And there are olives, feta cheese, pickled red cabbage, hard-cooked eggs, and rings of ripe melon.

Main dishes come with rice, crispy-roasted potato wedges, and a pleasant fresh salad. The izmir pilich is a deboned chicken leg, marinated, grilled, and fragrant with lemon. The "shish seafood" is three long skewers of nicely grilled shrimp, brightened with wedges of onion, tomato, and red and yellow peppers. Onions and vibrant-coloured peppers are scattered over the chunks of mostly fork-tender lamb (there was the occasional chew) in the "yogurtlu chep kebab." A thick, tangy layer of yogurt tops the assembly, and pita bread lies beneath.

For dessert, there are the usual Greek-Turkish pastries (like baklava and kataifia), and a milky custard topped with coconut and pistachios.

LITTLE TURKISH VILLAGE
2095 St. Joseph Blvd. (at Grey Nun)
(613) 824-5557
Access: One step at entrance; washrooms are accessible
Prices: Main dishes $5.95 to $12.95
Open: Lunch Tues.-Fri.; dinner Tues.-Sun.; closed Mon.

LUXE BISTRO

★★ ½   New American $$$

Found on the footprint of the old Le Crêperie (later renovated and renamed 47 York), Luxe was opened in June 2003 by the Firestone family— who also own Blue Cactus at the end of the block. After three-plus years as head chef at Social, Derek Benitz now helms the new Luxe.

There are decidedly modern updates, but Luxe reminds me of a men's club of a bygone era: a handsome, opulent room, outfitted with polished mahogany-coloured wood, large mirrors, tall potted plants, leather seats, black-and-white photos, elegant curves of bar and bench, and a collection of pretty long-haired women in nightclub uniforms.

Flesh, in various enticing forms, is a big draw here. Lots of meat on the menu: four cuts of superior steak (with your choice of potato and sauce) along with steak-frites, burgers, ribs, osso bucco, rack of lamb. Plenty of seafood, too. To start: oysters, shrimp cocktail, a seafood platter for two, and then mains of salmon, tuna, mussels, and bouillabaise. A small pasta section and a slightly bigger selection of large salads rounds out Benitz' wares.

A Luxe lunch reveals just how substantial those salads are—for $13, the niçoise is a steal, since this fish has never seen the inside of a can. Five thick slices of perfectly rare, sushi-grade tuna rest on the classic elements of this French salad—new potatoes, green beans, black olives, a hard-boiled egg (cleverly, quail). Beneath it all is a bed of bouncy greens. A delicious lunch, particularly when preceded by a French onion soup of exceptional quality.

Also very fine is the corn chowder, with its nubbly texture and its exotic infusion of toasted cumin. This is followed, however, by a disappointing sandwich: a grilled-vegetable panini, the bread moistened with a pesto mayonnaise and dollops of good goat cheese, but filled with vegetables that are no more than softened. Absent are the promised grill flavours we crave.

Our questions about the dinner menu are answered with authority by our server. He steers us toward the scallop starter. We will tip him well for this, for these are quite fabulous — three fat, perfectly-seared sea scallops are wrapped in crisp pancetta, set in a lime- and orange-scented butter sauce with a punchy tomato jam on top. And then two disappointments: a sweet-and-sour egg drop soup that is uncomfortably sweet, the sour balance undetectable; and then an unsuccessful tomato salad. This is tomato season, to be sure, but the dish is somehow flavourless, set in a sticky balsamic reduction that's too far reduced, too sticky-sweet.

Some better luck with the mains: Benitz buys beautiful beef and grills it well. His filet mignon is exceptionally good. His osso bucco is spoon-tender, rich marrow intact, explosive with a forceful gremolada — the traditional garnish of garlic, parsley, and lemon juice given a twist here by the substitution of orange and lime for the lemon. The veal shanks are set on a rich bed of creamy risotto and napped with a wine sauce that is dark and luscious. One slip-up is an overcooked salmon, though the fish is moistened well with a fine beurre blanc.

The apple tart is decent pastry, fashioned with slightly sour fruit, which takes well to the caramelizing and to the excellent cinnamon gelato. Far less successful is the chocolate mousse cake — the dark chocolate layer wimpy, the white chocolate layer spongy with gelatin. The maple crème brûlée has a curdled custard beneath its crackling surface.

Champagne cocktails and martinis have a prominent place on the liquor list. The wine list is not long, but well balanced in terms of price and origin — and with some interesting choices in the $30 range. About a third of the wines listed are available by the glass or quarter-litre.

LUXE BISTRO
47 York St. (at Byward)
(613) 241-8805
www.theluxe.ca
Access: Two steps at entrance; washrooms are small
Price: Main dishes $12 to $36
Open: Daily for brunch/lunch and dinner

MAMMA GRAZZI'S KITCHEN

★★   **Italian** $$

Mamma Grazzi's occupies two floors of a heritage building in the courtyard of the Byward Market. It's a homemade pizza and hand-made pasta kind of place, with a few salads and a few "secondis," and that's what it does.

A Mamma lunch might begin with a bowl of salmon and leek soup, finished lightly with cream and heavily (too heavily) with pepper. Then a Caesar salad, always a good test of a kitchen's worth—this one is full-bodied and bright. You should follow with pizza, one of a dozen offered, for the crust is chewy-crisp and what tops it is tasty. Ours is charming, nestled with tomatoes, sweet onion, and fresh rosemary, spread with chunks of pancetta, crisp rounds of paper-thin potatoes, and finished with sharp Parmesan. The pasta Katrina is a bowl of spinach spaghettini tossed with chunks of moist chicken, prosciutto, red onion, and black pepper-corns. Again, it's uncomfortably heavy on the pepper.

A Mamma dinner starts with one hit, one miss. The grilled cala-mari are lively with grill flavours, the squid yielding, the salad beside it fresh and sparkling, the plate carefully assembled. The mussels are hit-and-miss in terms of quality, carelessly tossed into a bowl too small for their bulk, which leaves the (rather bland) tomato sauce unable to reach them all. The pasta puttan-esca is overwhelmingly salty, the error not so much in the sauce itself (although a lighter hand with the anchovies might help) as with the proportion of it to the linguine. Less sauce would allow the pasta to absorb less strikingly the natural salts of capers, olives, and anchovies, rather than being besieged by them. No complaints about the veal scallopine, though: tender meat, treated with rounds of pancetta, grated parmigiano, and served with excellent roast potatoes—crisp, herbed, nicely peppered.

The ricotta cheesecake is delicious: it's studded with toasted almonds and pistachios, gently cheesy, delightfully unsweet. We also like the panna cotta, with its garnish of poached pears.

MAMMA GRAZZI'S KITCHEN
25 George St. (at Sussex)
(613) 241-8656
www.mammagrazzis.com
Access: Many stairs to negotiate; washrooms are upstairs
Price: Pizza, pasta, and main dishes $8.95 to $15.95
Open: Daily for lunch and dinner

MAMMA TERESA

★★ ½   Italian $$$

From her gilded frame in the front foyer, Mamma smiles down at you. She stands head and shoulders over the portraits arranged around her, autographed memorials of those who have supped here. Chrétien is on the wall, looking relaxed, well-fed, and slightly larger than the cabinet ministers, actors, crooners, and sports stars. Still, he's a pipsqueak next to Mamma Boselli.

Son Giuliano runs the place now. And everywhere—from the pictures and framed letters, to the backslaps and handshakes, the kisses and invitations to join a table—it is clear he is much of what this place is about.

Tuesday night, a howling wind, thirty below with squalling snow, and Mamma's is jam-packed: the Minister of Defence is in the sun room, two private parties are upstairs, and there's a birthday party in the salon.

Ah yes, Mamma Teresa . . . a long-established Italian restaurant with a devoted clientele. Followers surely return here more for the personal attention they receive, for the comfort of familiar surroundings, or for the little rooms upstairs where deals can be brokered in private—not out of any real affection for the food. Right?

I'm not proud of the fact that I was expecting ho-hum, but there you have it. True confessions of a constant eater.

What a pleasure to be so wrong.

The quality of the cooking at Mamma's is impressive. Not everything was right at our January dinner here, but there is nothing complacent about this food.

This is not a fancy place. Yes, the staff wear black-and-white uniforms and the dining happens in a series of rooms scattered throughout a lovely old house. But winter coats hang from hooks spread around the pale walls, dangling light bulbs are shaded with wicker baskets, the wall-to-wall carpet is industrial and worn, and the table settings seem commercial-grade. A kitschy collection of souvenirs, gadgets, curios, and ornaments lines the shelves.

All to say Mamma Teresa's has the feel of a busy home, rather than a designer eatery. And clearly, from the popularity of the place, nobody misses the Limoges.

Lunch began with tender, toothsome calamari. Then a superior tortellini in brodo, the broth robust, the veal-stuffed pasta pockets perfect, the seasoning just right. Mamma's Caesar is excellent. Ditto for her gnocchi. If your experience with these potato dumplings extends to the supermarket package, order a plate of Mamma's. They're light, tender, not the least bit gummy, full of potato flavour, bathed in the bold and lively house tomato sauce. Cannelloni (stuffed with cheese) and manicotti (with veal) arrive together, wrapped in sheets of al dente spinach pasta, pampered with more of that good sauce, and baked with a layer of cheese. A delicious berry cake features blackberries, raspberries, and red currants with custard and almond paste.

Dinner at Mamma's is not as uniformly impressive. A carpaccio starter is a mess on the plate — flavourful and cut to order, but carved badly, in scrappy bits, some thick, some thin, none of it pretty. And the halibut is overgrilled and dry. But here is toothsome, tender veal treated with a rich, basil-strong pesto sauce, served with roasted potatoes, deep-fried zucchini, and undressed steamed spinach. And the house tiramisu is one of the booziest in the city. Skip the après-dinner liqueur and slurp up a rectangle of this stuff.

Mamma's wine list is short and needs updating: twice I've tried to order a listed wine that's out of stock. If there is a special vintage list somewhere, they don't show it to us. Only the house wine is available by the glass.

MAMMA TERESA

300 Somerset St. West (at O'Connor)
(613) 236-3023
www.mammateresa.com
Access: Five steps into restaurant; washrooms are upstairs
Price: Main dishes $11.95 to $30
Open: Lunch Mon.-Fri.; dinner daily

MATSU SUSHI

★★   **Japanese**   **$$**

It has a bit of a Japanese rec room look, with its wall-to-wall carpet, pine panelling, and white walls. Paper lanterns hang from its ceiling, and homemade curtains shield four private cubicles from the rest of the square space.

There are fifteen tables spread around the room, laid with red-and-white cloths. At the far end, the sushi bar is supported by half a dozen stools.

But what this place lacks in ambience, it makes up for in big-heartedness — provided by two women who seem to delight in the business of pleasing you.

They also giggle a lot — with you, with each other, with the chef (and at least once with our table over the fact they'd forgotten the rice, tee hee hee . . . too funny).

Perhaps the mood would be altered or the laughter made less easy were the room busy, but on neither occasion I dined here did we have to compete for the attention or affection of these lovely women.

The menu offers the usual narrative, with fun thrown in: ika kara-age, Japanese-style cuttlefish, promises that "calamari lovers will never look back." It also offers the Korean-inspired dish of shaved beef, sweet and pungent, served sizzling hot with a side of kimchi (spicy fermented cabbage).

They make a restorative miso soup here. If you want something more potent of oceanic flavour, have the seaweed soup. Gyoza dumplings are delightful mouthfuls of lightly spiced pork stuffed in soft, white wrappers. A mere suggestion of a batter clings to the tempura shrimp and vegetables. The tatsuta age is fried chicken in a well-flavoured marinade of sweetened soy sauce and sake.

The star of the mains is salmon, presented in a black lacquered box, fresh, soft and moist, mingled with shredded seaweed, and topped with salty pink salmon roe. The disappointment is the tough steak teriyaki, sticky in its over-sweet sauce. The rest of the dishes fall somewhere in between. Udon noodles in broth are fine, but the shrimp tempura topper should be shrimp only, untainted by fake crab stick. Yakitori is tender dark meat skewered with on-ions, moist and fruity in its sticky sauce of soy, mirin, sugar, and tamarind. Sometimes these dishes come with iceberg, sometimes with greener greens.

Both the green tea and the red-bean ice cream are satisfying end-ings.

There is Japanese beer and sake, both good with this food.

MATSU SUSHI
175 Lisgar St. (at Elgin)
(613) 236-2880
Access: Steps into restaurant; washrooms are downstairs
Price: Main dishes $8.50 to $25
Open: Lunch Mon.-Fri.; dinner Mon.-Sat.; closed Sun.

MEKONG

★★   Chinese – Vietnamese $

We are regulars here. With flushed cheeks and tuqued heads, we tend to arrive après ski, goggles dangling, hungry, weary and in need of a fill-up. I've been let down by my children here, but never by the food, the service, or the bill.

Despite the frenetic pace of the packed dining room (with a healthy queue right out the front door), we find the spirits high and the attitudes kind among the Mekong staff.

One dinner, our table is in the big red room on the first floor. A second meal is taken upstairs, in a recently created attic room, the beams painted a cheering yellow, the narrow room framed on both sides with long stretches of upholstered bench and many white-and-red-linened tables in between.

We aren't wildly experimental at Mekong: wonton soup, spring rolls, Hunan dumplings, sizzling beef — it's a please-'em-all order we tend to place, with a few fish favourites and a peppery Szechwan dish slipped into the mix.

The chicken saté is luscious, its peanut sauce packed with peanut flavour, fired up with chillies. The pot stickers are fried-on-one-side dumplings of seasoned pork — very fresh, quite addictive. Steamed broccoli is crisp, green, bathed in the slightly salty, slightly fermented black bean sauce.

The house specialties are seafood dishes. Steamed salmon with ginger and shallots is reliable, as is the five-spice shrimp, the sauce pungent, fragrant, sweet, and spicy, the shrimp clean and crunchy. Braised duck is soft meat and vegetables in an aromatic, slightly sweet broth.

Mekong's curry dishes tend to be weak, tasting of powder—all heat without depth. The hot-and-sour soup has a thick texture, but a thin flavour. The wonton soup suits the lads better—a tasty homemade broth, barbecued pork slices, more of those good dumplings, and slippery Chinese greens.

There are imported beers and draft beer, and there is hakutsuru sake. Two dozen wines are available, five by the glass.

MEKONG
637 Somerset St. West (between Bronson and Percy)
(613) 237-7717
www.mekong.ca
Access: A number of stairs into restaurant; washrooms are small
Price: Main dishes $7.95 to $17.95
Open: Daily for lunch and dinner

MERIVALE FISH MARKET SEAFOOD GRILL

★★   Fish $

A mural tells the fishy story of this market family in vibrant co-lour. In the corner, Luigi and Christina are filleting fish. Their four children, two of whom run this café and fish store, are part of the harbour landscape too — as are the grandchildren, whose names grace the sides of fishing boats. It's a lively, whimsical scene by artist Sharon Pretty, and it dominates two walls of this homey fish store–café.

The chequered blue-and-white theme remains, but the fishing nets and plastic crustaceans hanging from the ceiling have been shed. And that's okay. The Coke machine that used to usher you in has been shifted to the far side, a bar has been built, and a simple wine list has been created. That's okay, too. The seating has been expanded as well: there's now space for about forty to feast on spanking-fresh fish, steamed, grilled, battered, breaded, brochetted — your choice.

This food is not without its disappointments. The shrimp and crab spring roll is mostly cabbage, fleshed out with a couple of baby shrimp and some artificial crab; and the calamari debases fresh, tender squid with a soggy, salty breading.

But there's more to please. Start with the house chowder, brimming with clams and root vegetables in a thyme-flecked creamy bisque; or the excellent mussels marinière, loads of very fresh-tasting mus-sels steamed to just-open in a simple, flavourful broth.

The fish and chips are fabulous: three fat fillets of halibut, moist and rich in a browned-up batter. Or go for the grilled salmon, or the salmon brochette, with big chunks of the succulent flesh in a gingery marinade. The fish entrées come with a choice of good home-cut fries or salad (nice greens that could use a better-quality dressing). There is Caesar salad with bouncy romaine, homemade croutons, fresh bacon, and a mayonnaise-y dressing that's gloppy but tasty enough.

And if nothing on the menu grabs you, head next door and point to a fish that appeals. They'll pull it off the ice and cook it for you—the marlin, perhaps, or a fillet of the (now ubiquitous) tilapia, or a chunk of fresh tuna. They're a cheerful, obliging bunch here.

Your kids will love the desserts—super-sweet, gummy, pre-frozen. I've learned my lesson: I order the chocolate death cake (or some such title) for the lads, and I eat leftover fries for dessert.

MERIVALE FISH MARKET SEAFOOD GRILL
1480 Merivale Rd. (near Clyde)
(613) 723-2476
Access: Fully accessible
Price: Main dishes $9 to $17
Open: Lunch and dinner, Mon.-Sat.; closed Sun.

NEW DELHI

★★★   Indian $

The hand that blends and roasts the spices at the New Delhi restaurant has a sure touch. The intoxicating aromas of those toasted Indian spices welcome you at the door of this handsome Glebe restaurant.

Here you are offered a variety of dishes from throughout the subcontinent. You can compare the red chilli–hot Madras with the rich, mild, sweetly spiced flavours of the Muglai curries. Or contrast the sour, acidic power of the mighty vindaloos with the Balti-style curries from the North-West Frontier and the Kashmir Valley. It's a tasty education.

Deep-fried starters are impressive. Order a round of onion bhaji, and you'll be rewarded with freshly fried fritters of tangled sweet onion scented with fresh cilantro coated in light and crusty lentil-flour batter. The samosas are triangular turnovers of pastry filled with gently seasoned vegetables. The New Delhi's mahkni soup has a rich flavour, creamy texture, and a mild but not insignificant spice heat.

Fresh Digby scallops are featured on this menu: sag scallops are buried in a spicy, well-oiled spinach mash; scallops pathiya are hotter, sour with lemon, sweet with coconut and garam masala. The classic butter chicken features firm meat, cooked slowly in a sauce of sweet and tart yogurt, rich with ghee and cream, garnished with raisins and nuts. Bhoona beef is a glossy brown stew, assertively flavoured with onion, ginger, chilli, black mustard seed, and cumin. Lamb korma is cooked in coconut with mild, sweet spices, the meat soft, the sauce beautifully fragrant, heady with chopped cilantro.

Of the vegetarian offerings, the mutter paneer and the baigan bharta stand out. The first is a mash of sweet-spiced peas with chunks of solid Indian cream cheese; the other is an aromatic eggplant paste, perfumed with cilantro. The basmati rice dishes arrive fluffy, fragrant with saffron, dotted with fruit and nuts, and strewn with softly fried onion.

Condiments arrive with all of this — a fiery chilli sauce, a pungent lime pickle, a bowl of sweet mango chutney, and the deliciously cooling, soothing raita. It's part of the fun of this food — customizing each bite to suit the palate and the mood.

Have the house rice pudding for dessert — cooked in cardamom-scented milk, strewn with nuts and served at room temperature — it is just the thing.

NEW DELHI
683 Bank St. (at Clemow)
(613) 237-4041
Access: Fully wheelchair accessible
Price: Main dishes $6.95 to $14.95
Open: Lunch Mon.-Sat; dinner daily

NEW MEE FUNG

★★ ½   **Vietnamese** $

It has taken me a few years, but I do believe I'm getting the hang of ordering from a ten-page Vietnamese menu. I don't, for instance, order a starter of Vietnamese spring rolls — because they show up over and over again, for no apparent-to-me reason, as embellishments on countless other platters of food. I've learned that pho — Vietnamese noodle soup — is not an appetizer. It's a bathtub-sized, every-food-group-accounted-for meal in a bowl. And I've learned to stay away from any item called "mock." Still, for all my hard-gained wisdom, I always (inevitably, invariably, and without fail) over-order.

This is a large, comfortable, but hardly memorable-looking space, known as the "new" Mee Fung ever since the "old" Mee Fung migrated to Booth Street from its former (puny) space on Somerset. "New" some eight years ago. The service is sometimes sweet and usually speedy, but don't count on much assistance with the menu — no time, no inclination. What you *can* do here with a fair degree of confidence is close your eyes and point, for nothing will disappoint.

We start with a round of Tsing Tao beer, and then get straight down to the business of over-ordering.

The business begins with paper and pencil. You record the dishes you want using the number system. Our lucky number is #223, lemongrass chicken: moist thighs, topped with a spicy homemade tomato sauce, sprinkled with shaved lemongrass, coriander, green onion, spread out on a base of sweet, fragrant rice. The dish with the most kick is the spicy saté with rice noodle (#136) — tender chicken again, bathed in a peanut sauce of great heat and flavour. The pork on the wrap-and-roll platter is exceptionally good. Moist strips of the sweetly barbecued meat arrive with shrimp, soft vermicelli, roasted chopped peanuts, grated carrot and daikon, bean sprouts, lettuce, fresh basil, and chopped cucumber. All of it, or some of it, gets layered on a round of softened rice-flour "paper," rolled up and dunked in a sauce of nuoc cham. That's a concoction built on a base of nuoc mam — Vietnamese fish sauce — with the addition of spices, carrots, sugar, vinegar. It makes for a good, fun, tasty bundle, particularly lively for the fresh basil within.

Vietnamese salads are not chilli-powered mounds of freshly grated raw vegetables and fruit, as they are in the Thai tradition. This goi is green papaya, carrot, and chopped basil, dressed with lime, nuoc nam, sugar, and vinegar, and topped with thin strips of sweet dried beef.

The dumplings are fashioned out of rice flour, stretched thin, filled with a minced meat mixture, steamed, and dipped in nuoc cham. The spring rolls are tasty, the deep-fried tofu fresh, judiciously fried, and quite delicious. And the beef noodle soup is a magnificent basin, the broth sweet and intensely fragrant, perfumed with coriander and basil, pungent with fish sauce, sharp with lime juice, and loaded with slices of rare beef, green onion, carrots, bean sprouts, vermicelli. Yum.

NEW MEE FUNG
350 Booth St. (south of Somerset)
(613) 567-8228
Access: Two steps into restaurant; washrooms are on main level
Price: Main dishes $5 to $12
Open: Lunch and dinner every day except Tues.

PAPAGUS

★★   Greek $$

It's nothing from the curb—a square white brick building of no particular appeal—but you enter to the warmest of greetings from owner Ted Karidis. Then you're surrounded with such exuberant, knowledgeable service that you're instantly taken with the place.

On this exhaustive menu—which has not changed since Papagus opened a dozen years ago—you'll find typical Greek fare: two dozen hot and cold appetizers, salads, vegetarian dishes, moussaka, quail, chicken, pasta, pork, veal, beef, seafood and, at centre stage, lamb.

There are combination platters and side orders and Greek feasts for two. There are Greek wines and Greek desserts and Greek music and, on the clay-coloured walls, frescoes of the guardians of the Cretan temple of Minos—creatures with peacock tops and lion bottoms.

It's all a bit much. Order a half-litre of the house wine, a very drinkable full-bodied Greek red, and ask questions. Let the Papagus servers guide you. They have been raised on this food since mother's milk lost its appeal. They have opinions. Our grinning waiter, a complete charmer, leads us toward the loukaniko, a Greek sausage of pork, garlic, oregano, and orange rind, grilled and sliced into thin disks of grand flavour. Melitzano salata is a delicious mash of baked eggplant mixed with garlic and lemon, thickened with olive oil. The spanakotiropita of spinach and feta baked in phyllo triangles is fresh; the gigantes (big butter beans) are meaty in a nondescript tomato sauce.

Better is the sauce that bathes the shrimp—a few big ones, slightly overcooked, tainted somewhat with iodine, but in a fine tomato sauce enriched with generous chunks of creamy feta. One enormous square of that good feta tops the house salad, dressed simply and effectively with oil, lemon, and oregano.

Turns out I'm more a fan of the starters than of the main dishes. The lamb souvlaki could be more tender, the chicken "riganato" could be more moist, and the à la carte fish selections could be fresh, not frozen. But they make a very good moussaka here, and I like the lamb with potato and cheese (featuring the ubiquitous feta and the hard kefalotiri cheese) dampened with that same fragrant tomato sauce, wrapped in layers of flaky phyllo, and baked to brown.

The deep-fried squid can be ordered to start, but also as a main dish in which the tender rings are lightly battered and fried up well, served with Greek salad and scorthalia, a chilled dip of mashed potatoes whipped with oil and garlic.

Finish with a shot of strong Greek coffee and a triangle of baklava, not too syrupy, strong of walnuts.

PAPAGUS
281 Kent St. (at Cooper)
(613) 233-3626
Access: Steps into restaurant; washrooms are downstairs
Price: Main dishes $13.95 to $29.95
Open: Lunch and dinner Mon.-Sat.; dinner only Sun.

PENSTOCK

★★ ½   **International** $$$$

This Wakefield mill has changed hands and purposes over its 166-year history, but since 2000 it has operated as an inn and a retreat in the hands of its keepers, Lynn Berthiaume and Robert Milling. There are stories, of course, of the life and times of such a building. Some of them are written on the menu; the more interesting ones you'll hear from the staff.

The Penstock dining room is one floor down from the main entrance. A window seat allows a view of the thunderous falls. In the gentle seasons, a deck offers a more immediate view, but in November, we're inside, in a busy room of large groups, at a table by the central fireplace. The crew of pleasant servers is kept running by the needs of these tables. The pace of our meal is "leisurely," with nearly an hour between starter and main dish. Water flows into our glasses at regular intervals, but the wine steward has long ago deserted us. We pour our own wine and we wait. Such is the pressure on a restaurant of a few big tables.

Happily, the food is worth waiting for. The last time I sampled the house smoked salmon, it was presented on rösti potatoes. This time the pale velvety slices, imbued with the earthy flavours of a gloriously good maple-wood smoking, are layered with deep-fried taro root moistened with a wasabi-infused sauce. It is magnificent. The spuds come with the duck this time, a dish in which thin rounds of the fried potato galette frame moist shreds of a luscious confit. Carefully chosen greens, tossed in a walnut oil vinaigrette, cuddle up alongside. We are happier with these two starters than with the chicken liver pâté, within which a piece of foie gras mousse is embedded. The texture pleases, but the flavour is too delicate, perhaps even dull.

My main dish is the featured sirloin. A thick slice of the blood-rare meat is thoroughly, gloriously infused with the smoky flavour of some fruity wood—apple? It is exceptional. Rarely have I tasted better beef.

There are lamb loins, roasted to medium-rare as requested, crusted with garlic and herbs. Sliced into thick slabs, the loin is served with cumin-scented carrots and a wedge of polenta, which in turn supports sautéed spinach and a fragrant ratatouille. Delicious. The one letdown is the rabbit bourguignon. The rugged sauce we expect is more a light glaze on this saddle, and although the meat is moist, the flavour is too mild. The duchesse potatoes seem wrong for this stew as well. And where are the mushrooms?

A hard, dense chocolate ganache is tough to cut. But once you get bold and stab it a few times, your efforts are rewarded, for this dessert has a crispy texture and dark, deep chocolate flavour, served with a tiny blob of ice cream that is utterly luscious. Ditto for the caramel drizzle. We want more. The crème brûlée is dreamy. The cheesecake is rich and superior. The poached pear is perfect. An excellent ending.

The Penstock wine list is an admirable document, with a wide selection of mostly French wines.

PENSTOCK
Le Moulin Wakefield (Wakefield Mill Inn)
60 Mill Rd.
Wakefield
(819) 459-1838
www.lemoulinwakefield.com
Access: Fully wheelchair accessible (elevator to dining room)
Price: Main dishes $18.50 to $31.50
Open: Daily for brunch/lunch and dinner

PERSPECTIVES

★★ ½   **Contemporary** $$$$

The white trunks of dozens of birch saplings frame the foyer of this handsome new dining room. They are lit from below with hundreds of mini-dots of pure white Light Emitting Diodes. LEDs are illuminated solely by the movement of electrons in a semi-conductor material. My high-tech dining mate suggests I should understand Ohm's law and the concept of dynamic resistance if I really want to grasp how they work.

I don't and I don't. Our diodes discussion reminds me that I'm in the heart of Silicone Kanata. Here to eat. That much I can grasp.

Perspectives is the restaurant of the swank Brookstreet Hotel, owned by high-tech entrepreneur Sir Terrence Matthews. It opened in June 2003, and its fall menu is the creation of executive chef Michael Blackie, just back from his last job in Bali. It reflects his experience cooking overseas — mostly in the Asia-Pacific region — as well as his obvious interest in working with regional products. You will find luxury ingredients and creative seasonal pairings on Blackie's dinner menu: foie gras with a mango-and-star-anise compote; carpaccio of tuna with local beets, apples, and a Veuve Clicquot "drizzle"; Ceylon tea–crusted salmon.

Sommelière Stephanie Monnin will pair Blackie's five-course "blind" menu with wines that match. She is gracious, professional, an asset to this room. As is the list she manages: still growing, it currently offers about a hundred selections from a variety of regions, in a price range of $40 to $340. In contrast, most of the servers are fairly green. Perhaps by the time you read this, they will be better-trained and more informed about the food they serve.

The blind menu begins with a disappointment—a pineapple, orange, and yam soup that is uncomfortably sweet—and then redeems itself with oysters: three Malpeques served with a pleasant chilli vinaigrette. A so-called granité (a granular ice made with flavoured syrup) is course number three. It turns out to be luscious green tea ice cream—fabulous stuff, but a palate-duller rather than cleanser. But the meat arrives, a juicy sirloin, its surfaces treated with a crackling coat of spices, including a comfy amount of lip-tingling spicy heat.

À la carte: a lobster bisque of exceptional flavour, within which floats a bronzed wonton-wrapped package oozing roasted garlic and creamy goat cheese. Next, a carefully made wild-mushroom risotto mounted with truffle oil. Plain roast chicken is a great test of a kitchen. Full marks for this bird of grand flavour, moist and juicy, infused with the rosemary with which it is cooked. It is surrounded with roasted-to-molten fingerling potatoes and slightly underdone green beans. On the side, a sauce of pan juices reduced with fennel seed and rosemary is pleasantly aromatic but also uncomfortably sweet.

Some dishes come with vegetables, some without. There is a short list from which you may select what you want: sage polenta, jasmine rice, baby beets, Asian greens, and others. I'm not a fan of this accessorizing: I want the kitchen to decide how my plate should be assembled. And they may be delicious sides, but I object to paying extra for them.

A lunch at Perspectives begins with the bittersweet, nutty-rich flavour of Jerusalem artichoke in a glorious soup. Then a delicate perch is paired with roasted plum tomatoes and greens dressed with a piquant vinaigrette. Perfect. The one trouble is with the saté-skewers of chicken, shrimp, and beef. They rest against a moist and aromatic brick of Indonesian-spiced rice, but these speared meats have had all their moisture and flavour sucked out from serious overgrilling.

Pastry chef Keith Matheson's desserts are presented in stunning arrangements. Ice cream and sorbets are homemade and swooningly good. There's a tarte Tatin, in which the featured fruit changes daily, and a warm molten chocolate cake that's almost (but not quite) too rich to finish.

Coffee arrives in little white pots, strong and good.

PERSPECTIVES
Brookstreet Hotel
525 Legget Dr. (at Solandt Dr.)
(613) 271-3555
www.brookstreethotel.com
Access: Fully wheelchair accessible
Price: Main dishes $24 to $36
Open: Daily for breakfast, lunch, and dinner

RANGOLI

★★   Indian $

Well, how 'bout that: a more-than-decent eatery in Orléans. Half-way between Jeanne d'Arc Blvd. and Place d'Orléans, on the ugliest strip of road in the region, neon letters in rainbow colours announce "Rangoli, Indian Cuisine and Sweets."

A benign pink-and-teal décor offers no allusion to the subcontinent. Even the poster art—including one of a golf course—and the whimsical roosters that line the bar at the back are pretty nondescript—left over, perhaps, from this address' earlier incarnation as a diner.

But the glorious smell of the place is unmistakably Indian, infusing and warming this plain, bright room of fifty seats.

We are served graciously, if a little hurriedly, while our server attends as well to those waiting for take-away orders to be packaged. We nibble our complimentary pappadum, order a round of mango lassi, and study the menu: here are all the deep-fried starters, curries, biryanis, tandoors, and vegetarian dishes that make up the usual north Indian repertoire.

Among the appetizers, the vegetarian samosas triumph over the salty ground-beef versions: fresh pastries packed with a seasoned potato-and-pea stuffing. The breast meat of the tandoori chicken is dry but the leg is beautifully juicy, subtly spiced. The onion fritters are mammoth, quite reddened with food colour, but still addictive. A tamarind dip tastes homemade, with all the bittersweet pungency of that fruit's pulp.

Mains arrive in copper vessels. The butter chicken is tender meat cooked in an exceptionally rich gravy layered with ginger and spices.

Cubes of lamb cooked with spinach (sag) arrive in a pretty pot, looking the colour of algae. The aroma of cloves and garam masala transforms the green glop into something glorious. The eggplant bharta is truly as good as it gets: a sensual, velvety mush of roasted eggplant singing with roasted spices. Large ovals of naan, flecked with black from the coals, browned, puffed and magnificent, are useful for mopping up.

Not all of it is glorious. The cardamom-strong gravy surrounding cubes of potatoes is delicious, but the spuds taste as though they were cooked a while ago. The sizzling platter of chicken wrapped in tandoori spices needs more than just a bed of raw onions to show it off. Not much finesse in the chicken biryani either; it is more a jumbled stir-fry than a distinctive layering. The rice, however, is fresh and fragrant; and the shrimp are big, crunchy ones, of a better quality and size than we are accustomed to getting in Indian eateries.

There is a refrigerator case filled with Indian desserts. The gulab jamun is authentically sweet. My French-Canadian companion, who grew up on sugar pies, loves these milky, buttery dough balls fried and soaked in a cardamom-infused sugar syrup. My teeth object.

Maybe not worth crossing town for—but if you live in the east end, relish this one.

RANGOLI

2491 St. Joseph Blvd. (at Dussere)
(613) 834-4549
www.rangoli.ca
Access: Fully accessible
Price: Main dishes $8 to $13
Open: Daily for lunch and dinner

RESTAURANT HÉRITAGE

★★★ ½   **French** $$$$

It rather leaps out at you, this solid square house from circa 1880, with its two levels of white balcony wrapped around a grey stone façade. For the past decade of its life as a French restaurant, the Héritage has been a pretty reliable dining option — though perhaps not worth the thirty-minute trip from downtown. But since 2001, when Serge Bélanger and his chef-partner Dennis DeRooy purchased this old house, it has become a pretty remarkable experience, and well worth the trek.

You will be graciously received in the handsome foyer, your coat whisked away before you are led inside. The main dining room is formal, the dark walls adorned with local art, the ceiling with a crystal chandelier, the space occupied by a dozen white-linen-decked tables. It's a luxurious room, but one in which you are instantly comfortable. For this you may credit the soft chairs, the thoughtfully spaced tables, the soothing music, but also the smooth, delightful service provided by Mr. Bélanger.

Chef DeRooy received his formal training at the Stratford Chefs School. His April menu is concise, embedded in the French classics, but not without some inventive twists. In addition to the à la carte menu, there is a four-course table d'hôte. From it, we begin with soup, a well-flavoured purée of celeriac and roasted pear. Next comes very fresh puff pastry, crisp and frail and buttery-rich, packed with a generous variety of wild mushrooms, soft chunks of venison, and guinea hen, in a full-flavoured, wine-enhanced sauce.

À la carte, you will do well to start with the shrimp cocktail. No jarred cocktail sauce for these three luscious shrimp: DeRooy has grilled some pineapple, boosted the sweet chunks with mango, balanced them with onion, and perfumed them with coriander. Then he's tossed in strands of pickled ginger for a rousing effect.

Not a disappointing nibble among the main dishes: a square of utterly fresh salmon arrives pink in places, darker pink in the centre, glistening with moisture, heady with a lively citrus vinaigrette, and served with a sweet red-onion confit. The rack of lamb, cut into three fat chops, is wondrous meat; its flesh tender, its surfaces treated with rosemary and buckwheat honey, the sweetness tempered with onion juices from roasted shallots that come alongside. A stuffing of cornbread, sweet peppers, roasted pumpkin, and pecans provides moisture and flavour inside a juicy breast of bronzed chicken, served with a yogurt sauce fragrant of star anise, cinnamon and cardamom.

The raspberry sorbet, made in-house, is tartly refreshing and of rousing raspberry flavour. The crème brûlée is textbook perfect. In the chocolate department there is a curious-looking construct of glistening brown which, when forked, reveals a dense, dark cake held together with a fabulously rich chocolate custard and coated with a thin (but not too thin) layer of chocolate ganache. In French, it's called "gâteau la boue." It is indeed delicious "mud."

The wine list is not long, but offers a selection from the New and Old Worlds—with space devoted to half-bottles for the light drinkers, and a page of options for the big spenders.

RESTAURANT HÉRITAGE
2607 Old Montreal Rd. (formerly Queen St.)
Cumberland
(613) 833-3000
Access: A ramp is available at the front door; washrooms are downstairs
Price: Main dishes $19 to $37
Open: Daily for dinner

RITZ ON CLARENCE

★★ ½   **Contemporary – Italian** $$

The food at Ritz on Clarence is in the neo-Mediterranean style — a kind of Italian with liberties — that is found over and over again in restaurants these days. There are the what-you'd-expect starter-ish things: the bruschetta, mussels, sautéed shrimp, salads. There's the "pasta fatta in casa" section, the list of wood-fired pizzas, and finally, the piatti completi — two chicken, two veal, two steak, two fish, one lamb, veggies, starch. You may have seen this before.

The difference is that what you see here is very good.

Go straight to the shrimp for a rich, comfort-food start: moistened in a vermouth-splashed cream sauce, pink and pungent with sun-dried tomatoes, garlic, and mushrooms, settled in a fresh puff pastry holder. Tender spinach greens are strewn with soft figs, crunchy pine nuts, and creamy goat cheese, the leaves wilting under a warm anointment of reduced balsamic vinegar and oil. It's a better salad than the Caesar, which sports a garlic, cheese, and mustard-rich dressing, but is mostly spine of romaine without enough of the leaves. The sweet-potato and shrimp fritters are an interesting idea, but come out dry.

The pasta calabrese is a pleasure — the full-bodied sauce is spiked with red wine, sweetened with soft onion, the sausage slices are moist and spicy, and the fettuccine is perfectly done.

The highlight of the mains is the veal, gloriously tender, treated with coarse mustards, onion, and tomato, laid over creamy mashed potatoes, and served with perfect carrots, beans, and broccoli.

Rapini, Italian sausage, and caramelized red onion top an excellent pizza crust, crowned with just a bit of cheese. The mahi mahi is overdone but rescued by the roasted garlic aioli and the awesome sauté of peppers, carrots, green beans, and spinach mingled with a concassé of saffron, fennel, tomato, and thyme .

For dessert, the Ritz's signature chocolate sabayon cake is about as satisfying a way of ingesting big-time calories as any I know.

RITZ ON CLARENCE
89 Clarence St. (between Parent and Dalhousie)
(613) 789-9797
www.ritzrestaurants.com
Access: Three steps from street; washrooms are accessible
Price: Main dishes $12 to $29
Open: Daily for brunch/lunch and dinner

ROMANO'S

★★   Italian $$

Romano Lelli is in the front of the house, and Biagio Provensano is in the kitchen. They've been an effective team for fifteen years, offering their Ottawa West neighbourhood a long list of northern-Italian classics designed to comfort and sustain.

There are fifteen appetizers on offer and just as many pasta and secondi dishes. In addition to the fixed menu there are daily specials, presented as a three-course prix-fixe package, with soup or salad, dessert and coffee.

The calamari fritti are marvelously tender. The leek soup begins with a superior broth and has sweet, gentle leek flavour; and the house salad is a pleasant plate of greens, dressed with sparkle, and stacked with slices of quality smoked salmon and properly just-cooked shrimp.

Next round: linguine with clams in a red sauce is perfectly cooked pasta tangled around many clams, slick with a tomato sauce that tastes of summer. Stuffed veal "Romano's" has been pounded and rolled around prosciutto and mozzarella, cooked beautifully and served with a rich sauce strong of cognac. The chicken "alla campagnola" is a plump, succulent breast sliced into thick slabs, set in a well-balanced white wine sauce with peppers, mushrooms, leeks.

The desserts are all in form. Of course, there is tiramisu, this version wonderfully balanced — the mascarpone cheese custard is just thick enough to further moisten the booze- and coffee-soaked cake; the whole of it pleasantly un-sweet.

In all, Romano's is a delight, not a dazzler — considered a personal favourite by many in Ottawa's west end.

ROMANO'S

309 Richmond Rd. (east of Churchill)
(613) 722-6772
www.romanos.ca
Access: Stairs into restaurant; washrooms are downstairs
Price: Pasta and main dishes $11.95 to $18.95
Open: Lunch Tues.-Fri.; dinner Tues.-Sun.; closed Mon.

ROSES CAFÉ ALSO

★★ ½   Indian $

There are two Roses in this city. Used to be three, but the Roses Café "Too" in Bells Corners has closed. That leaves the original Roses Café on Gladstone Avenue, and this one on Dalhousie Street in the Byward Market.

The atmosphere of this upstairs dining room is quite charming. The walls are painted red, yellow, and green, textured with cloths (wedding quilts) that swathe the ceiling. Tables are round glass, set with woven mats. Chairs are green metal, outdoor patio types. A bar dominates the back of the room. The front affords you a view of the Market from a lofty perspective. And I can't remember much about the floor — bare wood, I think — except that it was covered by a very impressive server.

Both the Roses Cafés deliver a spirited take on south Indian food, which means mostly racier masalas (curries) with pungent condiments designed to increase the depth of flavour. It also means you'll find a sizable vegetarian content on these menus. À la carte, the main list is surprisingly short, but blackboard specials fill in the gaps.

There is idli on this menu: small greyish-white "cakes" fashioned from a dough of ground rice and lentils, fermented and steamed and deliciously dunked in a coconut sambal. There are other options to rev them up — oily, dark sauces of intense heat. Your server will enlighten you. Pay attention.

The dosa is another classic southern treat, an extensive crêpe, slightly sour-tasting, crisp around the edges, soft in those places where the filling has soaked through. One dosa is stuffed with a mild curry of soft, sweet chickpeas, and the other with mushrooms and potatoes, fragrant of roasted mustard seed and coriander. Both are wonderful.

Mughlai eggplant is a glossy brown stew, cooked with onion, ginger, and garlic in a mild, sweet, yogurt-based curry pungent with cardamom.

You will find luscious butter chicken here, suffused with its coating of oven-charred ground spices. Soft chunks of lamb are embedded in fragrant basmati rice in one of the biryani dishes on offer.

Vegetarians will find sustenance and solace, for elaborate dinners can be built on the vegetarian offerings alone. Dhal is a thick and creamy mash of spicy lentils and complex flavours; baigan bharta is oily and rich, a paste of eggplant dotted with peas and tomato, perfumed with coriander; buttery spinach is dark and pungently seasoned.

I avoid the authentically, achingly sweet dessert offerings and finish happily with Indian tea, heady with cardamom and cinnamon.

ROSES CAFÉ ALSO
349 Dalhousie St. (at York)
(613) 241-8535
Original Roses Café is at 523 Gladstone (between Bay and Lyon)
(613) 233-5574
Access: Restaurant is on second floor
Price: Main dishes $7.50 to $16
Open: Daily for lunch and dinner

SAVANA CAFÉ

★★ ½   **Caribbean – Asian Fusion**   **$$**

I remember a visit to the Savana Café in April of 1999. It was during a heat wave—a week of gloriously warm, bug-free early spring weather—that had restaurants with decks scampering for outdoor furniture. I remember drinking rum punch and crunching kushi shrimp on the Savana patio, and toasting the wonder of an April-in-Ottawa evening spent in shirtsleeves. There was nowhere else we wanted to be. Good as the food was, these people could have served us fusion dirt and we'd have been delighted.

Three years later, April again, only this time I'm hanging up my parka on a hook . . . inside.

I will be harder to please.

The Savana Café has been dishing up its brand of tropical east-greets-west Caribbean-Thai-Vietnamese-Malaysian fusion cooking for twenty years. The décor has evolved a bit—matured, perhaps—but mostly it remains an intensely lush palette of colours, with vibrant art and toe-tapping music. It's a merry mood spread over the three rooms of an elderly Gilmour Street house.

The menu hasn't evolved much, either. Daily specials round out the à la carte offerings. Of the starters, the Savana mussels are the standout—perfectly cooked in a broth potent with lemongrass, basil, and mint, spicy with chillies and spiked with sake. The kushi shrimp are big guys, encased in a light tempura batter, studded with black sesame seeds, and fried up right. The sweet basil shrimp are bedded on coconut rice, pungent with a citrus-spiked oyster sauce and perfumed with Thai basil.

There is calamari, a mounded plate of battered and fried squid, tender and toothsome and served with a minted yogurt dip. Enriched with coconut milk, the kalaloo soup stays focused on the tart combination of okra, spinach, and lime juice.

Among the main dishes, we find the curry on offer delicious: an unrestrained dish of chicken with sweet potatoes and plantain in a potent sauce spiked with cilantro and chillies. There is also a very good jerk pork, its heat a pleasure, not a pain.

Two noodle dishes: a slightly too-sweet pad Thai, and somewhat overcooked soba noodles redeemed with yummy seafood in a spicy, sweet and pungent tamarind broth. The winning main is chicken, tender morsels in a hazelnut-studded cream sauce, rich with the flavours of wine, lemon balm, and thyme. Wilted collard greens and sweet-potato fries (both excellent) come alongside.

The house banana cheesecake with chocolate sauce is ridiculously delicious and comes with loads of sauce, which is exactly what you want.

You could drink any number of imported beers with this food, or a glass of guava juice, with or without rum.

SAVANA CAFÉ
431 Gilmour St. (between Bank and Kent)
(613) 233-9159
www.savanacafe.com
Access: Four stairs at entrance; washrooms are on main level, but small
Price: Main dishes $13.25 to $19.95
Open: Lunch Mon.-Fri.; dinner Mon.-Sat.; closed Sun.

SHANGHAI

★ ★ ½   Chinese $

Shanghai may be the oldest restaurant in Ottawa's Chinatown, but there's little sign of age. It is, in fact, a thoroughly modern eatery—hip and swank and mostly packed with Caucasians in sheepskin coats. A pillar in the middle of this moodily lit restaurant has been draped with mini–white lights and completely wrapped in white cloth. Through the cloth the lights blink on and off and on and off, and on and on and on. It's creative, if a bit distracting. Rather like the big, bold art on the red and yellow walls. There's no point in my describing it; by the time you read this, the collection will have been replaced with some other local artist's works. Suffice it to say there are no benign travel-agency posters on these wild walls.

I have never made it to Shanghai on a Thursday night, which may be a shame (I can't decide). A flyer advertises "Shanghai Beats Thursdays," with the music of DJs "Todd & Linus" accompanied by a "Happy Buddha Bar" of sake Caesars and Miss Zen martinis, and featuring dishes like sweet yam frites and "Mama Kwan's Bok Bok chicken wings."

The Shanghai restaurant belongs to the Kwan family, has since 1970. The second generation of Kwans runs the place now; one brother waits on us, the other one feeds us. The combination is quite delightful.

You can eat traditional Cantonese, Szechwan, or "other Asian" food here, or you can get the traditional goods with a nouveau twist. A starter of Shanghai dumplings is superb—the pork filling seasoned well, the wrappers soft, lightly fried, served with a hot chilli sauce that is more zesty and full-flavoured than spicy hot.

The "Hot or Not" Shanghai calamari is "not" for us, well-fried, soft, and crispy, and pungent with a black bean sauce. The peanut sauce on the coconut curry chicken is rich beyond belief, but eaten in moderation and mixed with lots of fragrant rice, it works just fine.

Better than fine is the "beef with Shanghai bok choy and roasted garlic." Slices of beautifully tender meat with bitter greens and caramelized garlic eat like a dream.

The shrimp in a spicy garlic sauce are fat and fresh, not a dud among them, mixed with crunchy, colourful vegetables. But the dish I eat and re-eat in my memory is the "spicy crispy fish with ginger sauce." Tilapia fillet dipped in a light tempura batter, judiciously fried, accompanied with sautéed shiitake mushrooms, peppers, onion, and doused in a ginger sauce of wonderful depth.

With all of this, some of us drink beer, and others have a glass of Henry of Pelham Baco Noir—fruity enough to stand up to some of Shanghai's strong flavours.

SHANGHAI
651 Somerset St. West (at Bronson)
(613) 233-4001 or (613) 233-4002
www.shanghaiottawa.com
Access: Steps at front door, better access at the side; washrooms are small
Price: Main dishes $9.95 to $16.95
Open: Lunch Tues.-Fri.; dinner Tues.-Sun.; closed Mon.

SIAM BISTRO

★★   **Thai** $$

Newcomers to this Westboro café may be attracted by its tidy white exterior, its bright blue awning, and the summer geraniums in its window boxes. But this bistro's clients are mostly regulars from the neighbourhood, drawn here by the citrus burst of lime leaves, the fire of chillies, the pungency of coriander, the searing sourness of fish sauce, and all the sensual perfume that is Thai cooking.

Without a reservation on a Sunday evening, we wait with those regulars.

Once seated at one of the round booths in this dark red room, we rev up the tastebuds with tom kha gai, plump with raw mushrooms and soft chicken in a basil-strong broth with all the right zing and zap and coconut-milk smoothness. Crunchy shrimp wrapped in rice paper rolls are judiciously fried, dunked in a sour-sweet tamarind-based sauce. The vegetable spring rolls are winners too, stuffed with black mushrooms, carrots, and cabbage, and packed with good flavour.

The green mango salad has all the innocence of a pretty, colour-packed plate, and all the searing spice and pervasive sour you want in a Thai "yum." The panaeng seems a relief now; its lusty sauce of thickened coconut milk and red curry is perfumed with lime leaf, basil, and crunchy with ground peanuts. Marinated grilled beef is presented in tender strips, suspended in a ginger-spiked broth. Rounds of crunchy-fried lemongrass crown the surface. It is magnificent. And the always-popular pad Thai is distinguished by its sweet and sour sauce — so slightly fishy, so slightly spicy — and by its fresh elements.

Tilapia fillets are doused in a ginger-strong, considerably milder yellow curry that's studded with potato. And back to the fire with a seafood curry: scallops, shrimp, and squid heated up with red-hot chillies, the whole deliciously perfumed with Thai basil.

There is Thai beer and lemongrass tea, of course, but this bistro also stocks a Pelee Island Gewürztraminer that works well with this complicated food.

SIAM BISTRO
1268 Wellington St. (west of Holland)
(613) 728-3111
www.siambistro.com
Access: Easy access into restaurant; stairs to washrooms
Price: Main dishes $8.95 to $12.95
Open: Lunch Mon.-Fri.; dinner daily

SIAM KITCHEN

★★   Thai $$

I've often been asked how I decide which restaurants to review. Does the *Citizen* tell me where to go? (No.) Do people send in suggestions? (Yes, thank you.) Do I have a roster of restaurants I re-review from time to time? (Yes.) And then there are chefs who move around, making an established restaurant feel new again. And of course, restaurants close and others open.

And then sometimes I lock my keys in the van, at lunchtime, just a half-block away from a restaurant I last reviewed in 1994. That's how this critic determined Siam Kitchen was next on the list.

Twenty-four years old, the Kitchen has the distinction of being Ottawa's first Thai restaurant. Opened in 1980 by Art Akarapan-ich, it showed Ottawa what lemongrass, lime leaves, galangal, and chillies could do for a chicken stock. It has changed owners a few times, and today, Siam Kitchen is in the good hands of Philip Lai and family.

Dark with teak-stained panelling and low-pile carpet, worn lower, Siam Kitchen occupies two rooms, both about the same size, with seating for fifty or so on hard wooden chairs. The tables are bare. The service is kind. The place smells good.

I order soup (hot, sour, sweet, fragrant with all the right stuff) just as the CAA guy arrives to restore me to my van. And then I return for the gang keow warn goong. There is considerable spicy heat in this fired-up coconut milk broth, but not so much that it cauter-izes the subtle anise flavour, the sharp fish sauce, the citrus thrill of lemongrass and lime leaves.

I return another day for dinner (my husband drives). We begin with the Kitchen's pretty ordinary fish cakes, served with a sweet and sour sauce of chopped cucumber and peanuts, mixed with chillies and scallions. The eggplant with tofu is fragrant with basil, and pretty with red and green peppers; zucchini and onions complement the chunks of purple-skinned eggplant and soft bean curd. The shrimp with cashews is short on cashews but long on flavour, with the shrimp mostly good (the odd mealy one appears).

The elements of a good pad Thai are all present and accounted for—noodles, shrimp, egg, peanut, bean sprouts—but the sauce that unites them is too sweet. The ginger flavour is strong in the pad King with pork; and the chicken wrapped in pandanus leaves are moist, flavourful nuggets, spiked with a spicy-sweet sesame dip.

SIAM KITCHEN
1050 Bank St. (at Aylmer)
(613) 730-3954
Access: No steps; washrooms are on main level, but small
Price: Main dishes $7.95 to $12.95
Open: Lunch Mon.-Fri.; dinner daily

SIGNATURES

★★★★   French $$$$

Think "Cordon Bleu" and pick out the anomaly: Paris, Tokyo, Sydney, London, Adelaide, Yokohama, Ottawa.

Trick question: there isn't one. This is the (slightly abbreviated) list of cities in which Le Cordon Bleu Paris now has a cooking school and related "Signatures" restaurant.

In Ottawa, a refurbished Sandy Hill mansion, refreshed with clean, vivid Provençale colours, boasts the only Cordon Bleu in North America. Opened with loads of whoop-de-do in the spring of 2001, Signatures occupies the front rooms, upstairs and down, of this grand old house. (The back is where the school part happens.)

Jackets, gentlemen, are required in the dining room. Ladies, your handbag will not be flung on the back of the chair — a cushioned stool is provided. Food arrives under silver domes in stunning arrangements (some might call them precious) — but once toppled and tasted, this is glorious food. As haute cuisine eating goes, there is nothing haut-er on the Ottawa side of the river.

Chef Philipe Filodeau has provided us with lots to read between the elegant blue covers of the Signatures menu — six pages of à la carte dining, followed by four separate tables d'hôte.

With a Signatures meal come freebies: an amuse-bouche to rev up the palate; a basket of wonderful bread; and always, at the end, a plate of fairy-tale fancies from the pastry kitchen.

At a spring dinner we begin with tiny crunchy rings of blanched asparagus encircling a herbed mascarpone filling, set in the centre of a deeply flavourful cream of asparagus soup. Circles of truffle oil sparkle on its surface. Seared foie gras arrives trembling pink and buttery, paired with a mix of wild mushrooms. Raw scallops are delicately sliced, moulded into a ring, anointed with coriander oil, and rested atop a fragrant cake of potato and leek.

The layer of fat beneath the deep, crisped brown skin of a roasted breast of duck is much responsible for the juiciness of this delicious bird. A red snapper arrives in its skin, fresh and firm under its crown of deep-fried leek. Beneath the fish is a "tian"—paper-thin rounds of potato atop a creamy, rich sauté of soft leek and potato. Fish and tian are set in a bitter sauce of puréed watercress. Wonderful. An utterly fresh piece of halibut glistens with pistachio oil, its flavour perked up by multi-layers of caramelized red onion, tomato concassé, and a green-olive tapenade. The French fruit-with-duck tradition is upheld with a sweet cinnamoned apple ring neatly buried within a meaty confit. Scattered around the plate are more wedges of soft, bittersweet apple.

Knowing that the darling plate of tiny meringue swans, spears of caramel, chocolate truffles, etc., is en route (and on the house), you could consider skipping dessert. Certainly the desserts are, like much of the food here, architectural wonders of immense fussiness . . . and who needs that? The trouble is, they're to die for. My green-tinted, soft-chewy-crunchy pistachio macaroon, topped with a layer of raspberries, a crown of pistachio cream, and served with a lemon verbena sorbet is—well, words fail me. I am light-headed just at the memory of the crunch, the smooth, the ice, the sweet, the tart.

It's also possible to become light-headed when you see the bill. Certainly it's not hard to spend $160 for two to dine here with a modestly-priced bottle of wine from a lengthy list. It includes bottles with big price tags, as you might expect, but also a number of choices in the $30 to $40 range.

SIGNATURES

453 Laurier Avenue East (at Range)
(613) 236-2499
www.lcbottawa.com
Access: Ramp is available; washrooms are accessible
Price: Main dishes $29 to $41
Open: Lunch Tues.-Fri.; dinner Tues.-Sat.; closed Sun. and Mon.
Dress code applies

SOCIAL

★★ ½   **Contemporary**   **$$$$**

There has been some change in this kitchen. Original chef Derek
Benitz has moved down the street to the new Luxe Bistro, and Rene
Rodriguez, late of the ARC Lounge, has moved in to helm the Social
stoves.

But the physical place remains as it was. Social is a strikingly handsome high-ceilinged room, in which the old stone walls and high
scalloped front windows work harmoniously with the new black
granite tables, high-backed rounded booths, au courant shades
of taupe, and a bordello-red padded partition — the one blast of
colour in the place, it works to divide the main dining area from
the long, curved bar.

I have been here for a midweek lunch and found myself in a lonely,
echoing room, and I have been here on a Friday evening when the
place was charged with energy.

Canadian-born, Mexican-raised Rodriguez brings to Social his
Mediterranean sensitivities. Bold Spanish flavours, Moroccan hab-
its of pairing the savoury with the sweet, and modern makeovers
of classic Italian dishes are evident on his fall menu.

The food here can be absolutely splendid. The gnocchi are gloriously soft, thimble-sized nuggets floating in a sauce rich with
mascarpone cheese and sweet with puréed chestnut. The seafood
chowder is gently but firmly flavoured, and generous with its perfectly cooked fishy offerings.

It can also be trying: an oversized plate for an undersized portion of foie gras seems wrong. The two mouthfuls are pleasant
enough — the liver crusted sweetly with gingersnaps, paired with a
somewhat-too-astringent jalapeño-spiked pineapple relish — but

it is silly-looking on such an enormous canvas. A starter of baked apples, quartered, spread with pistachios moistened with truffle oil and dollops of goat cheese, arrives lukewarm—the apples still quite raw, and going brown. I was expecting soft, cooked fruit. It would have worked better that way. A braised lamb shank with honey and pickled figs towers above the plate. The meat is admirably cooked and tender, but it is also uncomfortably sweet. The honey needs a savoury balance not quite provided by the lime-doused figs.

But there's more that works well. Linguine are perfectly cooked, swirled around marinated artichokes, crisp pancetta, bitter greens, and chopped sage; the only wrong note is the overcooked shrimp. A steak is flavourful, scattered with shiitake mushrooms, paired with a sweet-tart red onion marmalade, good frites, and a side of Caesar salad.

The lavender crème brûlée is properly rich, properly cooked, but the truth is—and I know it's just my particular problem—the lavender infusion reminds me too much of hand cream. I have no trouble with Social's chocolate sabayon, however: a generous portion (best to share) of fabulous chocolate mousse on a dense ganache crust, wrapped in chocolate leaf, served with slices of papaya and a good raspberry sauce.

There are many martinis and champagne cocktails on the drinks menu. The Social wine list is user-friendly, with descriptions and suggestions for matching wine to food. A generous selection of wines is available by the glass; and although there are a number of bottles with big tags, there are also good choices in the $30 range.

SOCIAL

537 Sussex Dr. (at York)
(613) 789-7355
www.social.ca
Access: Dining room, bar, and patio are fully accessible; washrooms are downstairs
Price: Main dishes $18 to $34
Open: Lunch Mon.-Fri.; dinner Mon.-Sat.; closed Sun.

STONEFACE DOLLY'S

★★ ½   Café – Eclectic $

The room is, to say the least, nondescript. There are some wee white lights strung over the open kitchen and some fun stuff is painted on the walls, but mostly this restaurant/pub has the look of an all-day-diner dropped into an un-happening neighbourhood. Before the food arrives, my Stoneface Dolly's dining mates are palpably anxious about the place, dinner-on-me notwithstanding.

But there is considerable talent and noble intention in this peculiar little place with the funny name. You find the talent both in the front of the house, provided by amiable owner Bob Russell, and in the kitchen, where his son Jeff performs fusion wonders in a minivan-sized space.

The funny name . . . yes, well, it concerns the previous owner's grandmother, who had a legendary reputation for a deadpan countenance at cards. I think I've got that right. I was only half-listening to the tale, distracted as I was by Dolly's wine list. Judging by its prices, it can hardly be lucrative, but it's an interesting document nevertheless. Given the look of the place, I was expecting to find Kressman by the glass. The house wine is, in fact, Pelee Island. Of the ten bottles on the list, three are Australian wines, four are Canadian, and three are from South Africa (Bob's birthplace). There's also a featured wine, a beer of the month, beer on tap, and a selection of microbrews.

The featured wine, a Stellenbosch Origin, is described as "the laughing, eating, talking, drinking, singing, sharing South African wine . . . for Canadians." It's crisp, fruity, off-dry, and works well with the day's soup—a gazpacho, coarse and ripe with summer's gifts, perfumed with coriander, sharp with lime juice, spiked with jalapeño. Slices of grilled foccacia bread, some spread with goat cheese and oily grilled eggplant, others rubbed with pesto and topped with ripe tomatoes and fresh basil, are devoured. My Other Mouths around the table begin to relax.

Dolly's warm vegetable salad reveals a talent with the grill: the peppers and onions are perfectly caramelized, their sweetness set on a platform of balsamic-wilted greens topped with a piquant tomato concassé and a round of potato-crusted goat cheese. Delightful.

Mussels are plump, fresh tasting, mingled with peppers, mushroom, garlic in a sweet, spicy, and sour Thai red curry sauce, smoothed with coconut milk.

Of the main dishes, the jerk chicken is magnificent, flanked with cardamom-scented basmati rice, a yogurt raita, a black bean and tomato salsa, and slices of roasted banana. I report on more ways with chicken because it so happens that four of the five main dishes feature the bird. I guess that's a criticism, but there you go. Chicken is infused potently with tarragon, paired with a pleasant portobello mushroom sauce, and set on excellent butter-bathed polenta. And then a pleasant pasta dish with chicken, vegetables, and grilled radicchio is bathed in a green Thai coconut curry. The roasted vegetables surrounding the salmon are grand, and the fruited couscous is fine, but the fish, unhappily, is overdone.

For dessert, try the lemon curd tart. The final flourish is the bill. Unless they've figured it out by the time you read this, it will be incredibly reasonable.

STONEFACE DOLLY'S
479 Bronson Ave. (at McLeod, just south of Gladstone)
(613) 230-2088
Access: Short steps at entrance; washrooms are small
Price: Pastas and main dishes $9.95 to $12.95
Open: Lunch Tues.-Sun.; dinner Tues.-Sun.; closed Mon.
Note: Beer and wine only

SUISHA GARDENS

★★   Japanese $$

At noon, hordes of downtown lunchers descend on this place. But if you come at one o'clock, you won't need a reservation; and by 1:45, the sushi chef is packing up his mis-en-place. At dinner, when the pace is more serene, the tatami rooms in the basment are favoured.

You enter Suisha Gardens to a long, dark foyer. You will be greeted warmly and directed to the coat check and; and if your reserved table isn't quite ready, you will not likely mind: the sweet woman who begs your indulgence for "just a little minute" is so darn cute.

The gracious Mike Arai arrives and leads you up a few stairs and into a spacious room, a sizable chunk of it occupied by the sushi bar and prep area. Water will arrive immediately. The servers seem puzzled as you mull over the menu. Most of their lunchers know exactly what they want: one of the eight combination plates Suisha Gardens has put together for the fast crowd.

If you don't know the basics of this food, head to the sushi bar and take a look at their wares. Along a conveyor belt of traditional wooden boats (Japanese junks) float little examples from the sushi menu, shiny with shellac. You point and the chefs will sculpt a similar-looking still life (from fresh material).

We sample a selectionof standard nigiri sushi: two pieces each of firm, succulent hamachi, tuna, salmon, and shrimp, and three California rolls. This plate of fourteen two-bite tasty treats costs $18.95. With a delicate bowl of miso soup to start, or a plate of hiyashi wakame (lengths of soft-chewy seaweed marinated with sesame oil and scattered with browned sesame seeds), it makes a very satisfying, filling lunch for about $12 each.

As for the cooked goods, the tempura is a generous, attractively towered assembly of shrimp, onion, carrot, squash, mushroom, and zucchini fried in light, crisp batter, dunked in a thin, sweet, soy-based sauce. Yaki-gyoza, Japanese (also Chinese) dumplings of lightly seasoned pork, are very fresh tasting, fried on one side, dipped in a sweetened, soured sauce. Thin-sliced pork, marinated in grated ginger, soy, and mirin, is grilled and propped up with rice. Green onions sprinkle the top and Japanese pickles are on the side.

Green-tea ice cream is a soothing way to close. Not that the bill will cause much concern. Unless, of course, you've gone overboard pointing at dozens of those junks.

SUISHA GARDENS

208 Slater St. (between Bank and O'Connor)
(613) 236-9602
www.japaninottawa.ca
Access: Many steps to negotiate
Price: Lunch combinations $8.95 to $12.95; complete dinners $12.95 to $25.95
Open: Lunch Mon.-Fri.; dinner Mon.-Sat.; closed Sun.

SWEETGRASS

★★★   **Aboriginal** $$$

Housed in an ex-sweets shop on Murray Street, Sweetgrass opened in November last year, distinguishing itself as Ottawa's first aboriginal restaurant (and purportedly Canada's second).

You enter to a bar area and open kitchen: a vibrant white, red, and black workspace where chefs/owners Phoebe and Warren Sutherland preside. The dining room is furnished with cool white linen and warm wheat colours, the textured walls decked with native art and artifacts. The background music is melodic, moody drumming.

It is an original experiment: bringing First Nations cuisine to Ottawa . . . with a wee nod to Jamaica.

Yes, Jamaica.

Indeed. It's what makes Sweetgrass a quintessentially Canadian restaurant. The story: a northern Québec Cree woman meets a Jamaican man at the New England Culinary Institute. After jobs in New Mexico, they open a restaurant together in Ottawa with offerings of Arctic char, buffalo steak, caribou sausage, and wild rice alongside Bounty rum bread pudding and pots of Jamaican Blue Mountain coffee.

The Sweetgrass winter menu is a short, appealing list of indigenous beasts, birds, and fish. It's rounded out with vegetables, grains, and fruits that make seasonal sense, prepared in creative ways by talented hands.

Dinner begins with a magnificent wild mushroom soup, aromatic with thyme and of good woodsy flavour. Bacon lends a pleasing smokiness to a hearty potato and corn chowder. The organic field greens sport a maple-mustard vinaigrette.

Navajo fry bread is the base for a comfort stew of wild mushrooms, the construct dotted with toasted pine nuts. Wedges of pickled sunchoke are supported by more of those good greens, treated with a cider dressing, and sweetened with honey.

Next comes a potato salad featuring purple and yellow fingerlings and soft-cooked quail eggs, all moistened with a coarse mustard dressing. Pink slices of tender smoked duck are paired with a wintry relish of cranberries and apples.

The house Riesling (Sweetgrass Harbour Midnight, Niagara Peninsula) works well with the fish cakes. These are big-time winners: rich with smoked flavour, but delicate and moist within a crisp shell. Caribou sausage, quail, and duck, united in a rich sauce, are the hunter's pot pie, spilling out of a buttery pastry shell topped with a layer of sweet, moist cornbread.

Dinner mains include a tender, juicy buffalo steak, a moist and perfectly grilled Arctic char, and a slow-roasted leg of Canada goose, the toothsome meat dripping off the bone into sautéed bitter greens, balanced with a sweetly-roasted root vegetable "hash."

The steak is escorted by wilted chard and firm potatoes, tangled with celeriac in a preparation au gratin. The char comes with an excellent wild rice pilaf.

For dessert, a warm slab of bread pudding propped up with Jamaican rum, vanilla ice cream, and a luscious caramel sauce; an expert crème brûlée infused with rosemary; and three slices of a dark, moist, currant-studded Cree cake called buudin, served with cream. The Blue Mountain coffee ($6) isn't strong enough for me. We enjoy the selection of native teas more.

If I could suggest two things: ditch the complimentary popcorn in the dollar-store bowls—it starts things off on a weak note. Offer a bit of bannock or wedges of that wonderful Navajo fry bread instead.

The Sweetgrass wine list offers a dozen choices of New World wines in the $30 range, along with a handful of more expensive wines from Italy and France.

SWEETGRASS
108 Murray St. (between Parent and Dalhousie)
(613) 562-3683
www.sweetgrassbistro.ca
Access: Stairs into restaurant; washrooms are small, but on main level
Price: Main dishes $18 to $28
Open: Lunch Mon.-Fri.; dinner Mon.-Sat.; closed Sun.

TAJ

★★   Indian $

I have a tale about Taj.

The ten-year-old boy next door wanted chapatis to share with his classmates for a project on the foods of India. So his mother called the Taj restaurant on Carling Avenue, explained her son's project, and asked if she could order a dozen for take-away. Mr. Bakshi explained that chapatis were not on his menu, that these flat griddlecakes were served mostly at home, but that his wife would be making some at noon. He would ask her to fry up a few extra.

Oh, goodness, she couldn't possibly trouble his wife.

No trouble, here were directions to his home. The chapatis were ready at noon; payment was refused.

Nice story. The point? Well, there isn't one. It's just a tale about graciousness and community-mindedness and going the distance. Needless to say, my neighbour is now a Taj regular.

Taj also distinguishes itself by the lustiness of its spicing, the long drenching of meat in marinades, its expertise with the white-hot coals of the tandoor, and certainly with the hospitality of its personable, chatty, and sometimes cheeky host.

From the tandoor, better the bird with the bone in, for the flavour is superior; but even the boneless chicken tikka is moist, marinated to deep red, expertly cooked. Eggplant is gloriously permeated with smoky, charred flavour from its time in the coals, mashed and mixed with soft onions, fresh coriander, and spices. The butter chicken is tender meat in a lusciously creamy, ginger-fragrant, tomato-tinted sauce. Strips of tender beef float within an appropriately searing Madras-style curry, fragrant of mustard seed, ginger, cumin, and tangy vinegar. The shrimp disappoint, however—mealy, tough, tiny ones buried in an aromatic purée of spinach.

Gulab jamun are rose-flavoured sweetmeats in a honey-sweet syrup, a taste I have been utterly unable to acquire. Others who have a sweeter tooth love this dessert. I find other stuff to love at Taj.

TAJ
3009 Carling Ave. (across from the Coliseum)
(613) 726-6955
www.tajindiancuisine.com
Access: Easy access into restaurant; washrooms are small
Price: Main dishes $8.95 to $16.95
Open: Lunch Mon.-Fri.; dinner daily

TAJ MAHAL

★★ ½   Indian $

If you live in the Glebe and fancy a curry, you're all set. On the dozen blocks between Pretoria and Holmwood, Bank Street now boasts four Indian restaurants. Taj Mahal anchors the collection at the bottom of the map, but for my money (and mouth), it rates closer to the top.

Picking the Taj Mahal was a fine decision. My mistake was coming here with both my husband and a woman who had lived and travelled widely in south central Asia (mostly on a motorbike, apparently . . .). This well-travelled, well-sated single blonde also happened to be—as I discovered mid-dinner—an old high-school flame of my husband.

That, to tell the truth, was the mistake part.

"Have you ever been to India?" she purred, eyebrows arched, as she noticed my pen, my notebook, her question aimed at the very moment I took a large mouthful of bhuna gosht.

"Hmmwellno . . . "

"Ahhh . . . pity."

My husband (who had also been to India) exchanged a sympathetic look with the blonde ex .

Perhaps the vindaloo would make her mascara run. (Apparently not. It only added to the glow.)

The appetizers were all wrong, too. The samosas, onion bhajia, and squid rings arrived over-fried and dry. Even the chutneys couldn't help them.

But the naan was absolutely splendid—browned, buttery, puffed ovals flecked with black from the tandoor coals. The palao rice was freshly steamed basmati cooked with peas, fried onions, and cumin seed, served for us on polished plates by a kind and accommodating serving staff.

Then the parade of stews arrived in small, deep serving dishes. Even The Blonde—who had had much evil to say about the squid—liked the salmon, thick hunks of moist fresh fish coated in a well-herbed yogurt-based marinade, potently flavoured, sizzling with peppers, onions, and lemon. The butter chicken was properly rich and comforting. Ginger livened the dhal curry, a mix of lentils in a pale brown gravy. The bhoona gosht featured cubes of lean, gloriously tender, and deeply aromatic lamb. The grilled eggplant was a wonderful dish, strong of ginger, cooked with tomatoes and onions and cayenne.

I tasted the vindaloo last. It was, like my dinner guest, adult in flavour, breath-robbingly-hot, and puckering-sour.

Soothe yourself with a Kingfisher beer.

TAJ MAHAL
925 Bank St. (at Holmwood)
(613) 234-1280
Access: One step from street level; washrooms are downstairs
Price: Main dishes $5.95 to $17.95
Open: Lunch and dinner daily

TAKARA

★★ **Japanese** $$

Takara is a bright corner restaurant in the Byward Market, found where Dalhousie meets George. The sushi bar provides the centre of attention. The rest of the room is broken up by square screens that create separate spaces among the twenty or so tables. The room is efficient, linear, and bright. The spotlight on our particular evening was turned on a duo of Ottawa's Finest, fortifying themselves with smoked river eel before returning to monitor the merrymaking of the toga-clad Ottawa U. frosh, tied together day care-style, parading the streets.

Sushi: the new snack food of the twenty-first century cop. Gotta like that.

Takara doesn't pretend to be anything but a simple Western-style Japanese restaurant, where you can get a complete nigiri sushi dinner, with soup or salad to start, for $14. And the food is pretty good here, in both its natural and treated states.

Sushi and sashimi are offered in all the most basic raw fish varieties. These Japanese canapés are fresh-tasting and carefully made. As for the cooked stuff, there are noodle soups (both udon and soba noodles), and the usual assortment of appetizers. The miso is a pleasant dashi stock clouded with tofu and dotted with spring onions. Gyoza are good, made of herbed ground pork in delicate noodle wrappers. Calamari fritti, Japanese-style, are quite wonderful: the strips of squid are tender, the batter light, and the results just greasy enough to be fun. Sunomono is a seafood-and-cucumber salad in a sprightly dressing of sweetened, gingered rice vinegar.

The tempura is a presentation of fried morsels of big, fat shrimp and vegetables (green beans, mushrooms, sweet potatoes, carrots). Not the most ethereal batter you've ever had, but fine nonetheless. The house salad is a routine plate of chopped iceberg, a slice of cucumber, a wedge of tomato, vaguely livened with a pickled-ginger-rice-vinegar-dressing.

Takara makes a fine teriyaki chicken, the meat tender, well-flavoured in its marinade of soy sauce, sugar, ginger, mirin, garlic, and sesame. Its steak is less fine—a New York cut that's thin, tough, and juiceless.

For dessert, there's good green-tea and red-bean ice cream.

TAKARA
366 Dalhousie St. (at George)
(613) 241-6582
Access: Two steps from street; washrooms are on main level
Price: Sushi and sashimi dinners $12 to $27
Open: Lunch Mon.-Fri.; dinner Mon.-Sat.; closed Sun.

THE MARSHES
BAR & GRILL

★★ ½   **International** $$$

Part ski chalet, part barn (with touches of Frank Lloyd Wright), this four-storey space is supported by soaring timbers, fleshed out with stone, pine, and wall-to-wall windows, and flooded with light. Depending on your perch—on the wrap-around patio, at the sleek bar, on commodious circular banquettes, or at one of the dozens of amber-brown tables—the view is either of the greens, the high-tech skyline, or the for-now-fallow fields to the north.

It's a fashionable space, certainly—designed and coordinated, yet casual too: you can come as you are and flop into it, allowing the button-down servers, name-tagged and keen, to wait upon you.

At dinner, this 230-seater is all but empty—just billionaire owner Sir Terry Matthews and his party; and, two banquettes away, me and mine. At lunchtime, the place is livelier. This is a room that needs filling, and (a few foodie quibbles aside), it is a room that deserves filling.

Chef Hector Jimenes (late of the Hilton in Boston) has designed a menu that attempts to please all. It offers the nachos, fired-up wings, and big fat steaks for the golf-club crowd (albeit with sides of taro chips). Then he raises the bar with less predictable fare like grilled scallops with melted chestnut butter, figs, and Himalayan red rice.

Often when a hotel or club restaurant tries to get all fancy-pants, it flops. That isn't the case here. You can actually overlook the standard grazing appetizers and be rewarded with the tasty innovations. So-called lamb lollipops are fabulous little two-bite chops, coated with mustard and cornmeal, grilled to rare and served with a mango salsa spiked with jalapeño. The tempura shrimp are impressive both for their size and for their snap-crackle-pop fresh taste; they're coated with a light, utterly greaseless batter, perched on a mound of crackling rice noodles, and served with a sweet, sour, and slightly spicy red pepper sauce. A crab soup is almost more a dip, it's so dense—pleasantly spiced and smoothed with cream. And then more crab in two solid cakes, cornmeal-dusted, firm, and tasty. They are equipped with an equally rich sauce that falls just short of overwhelming them with its potently smoky flavour.

Seafood is done well: mussels, scallops, and shrimp are quite perfect in a pasta dish of intense flavour and considerable spicy heat. Scallops again, but starring alone, are fleshy and yielding, perfectly grilled, supported with a moist mound of red rice. There is juicy chicken dished up with shiitake mushrooms, sweetened with a full-flavoured Marsala wine sauce; and there are mussels, poached in a comforting sauce of cream, wine, tomatoes, and tarragon, abetted with a saffron-coloured (but not scented) aioli.

The burger is a curious letdown—big enough, moist enough, but screaming out for seasoning. It's backed up with a black bean "relish" that amounts to little more than a can of black beans.

Desserts are a collection of too-sweet, too-rich, largely flavourless confections (cheesecakes with names like "turtle"), most of them baked elsewhere.

THE MARSHES BAR & GRILL
The Marshes Golf Club
320 Terry Fox Drive (near March Road)
(613) 271-3370
www.marshesgolfclub.com
Access: Fully accessible
Price: Main dishes $12.95 to $28.95
Open: Daily in summer (7 A.M. to 10 P.M.)
Winter: brunch/lunch only, Sun.-Fri.; closed Sat.

THEO'S

★★   Greek $$

I christened my new "stretch" trousers at Theo's Greek Taverna. If ever there was a restaurant where a woman needed a bit of give around the waist, Theo's would be the place.

It's been in the business of overfeeding people at its Richmond Road location since 1987. Found in the centre of a strip mall where Woodroffe Avenue meets Richmond Road, Theo's tall peaked roof sets it above the neighbouring businesses. Under that roof you find a lively, friendly room, painted pink, with frescoes of Greek scenes to Remind You of where you are. Theo's host and owner, Jerry Vamvakas, seems much the spirit of this place; he's a big fellow, handsome, amiable, and very present, greeting and seating, describing and advising.

He directs us to the option called "pikilia" (selecting any four appetizers for a thorough sampling). We choose the melitzano salata right off the bat, a superb dish of roasted eggplant peeled and mashed with onions, garlic, olive oil, a splash of red wine vinegar. Wedges of warm, herbed Greek pita are provided to transport this yummy stuff. And then meatballs, or keftedes, fashioned with lamb, fragrant with mint, charred on the outside, juicy on the inside, quite delicious. Shrimp are bathed in a garlicky, winy tomato sauce enriched with feta cheese. Our fourth sampler is the letdown—well-flavoured octopus that is much more of a chew than we want.

You could start lightly with avgolemono, a Greek classic, with chicken and rice in a thick chicken broth, well-livened with lemon. Or with a first-class Greek salad, fragrant with oregano, lemon, olive oil, loaded with feta, olives, onion, peppers.

Of course, there's always moussaka: made with beef, not lamb, but flavourful, the charred eggplant assertive, and the top of it happily *not* a thick goo, but a well-seasoned béchamel, browned and crackling. With it comes more of that very fine Greek salad. It is, for $11.95, a substantial and satisfying dish. The "surprise" lamb ("ezohiko") is tender chunks of lamb and potato slow-cooked with feta and kefalotiri cheeses, seasoned and herbed, topped with a tomato sauce, the whole of it wrapped in layers of phyllo. The weakness of the dish is the wrapping: the pastry is limp and soggy. A fillet of sole is weak too, the fish dry. But then a winner again: the chicken "Corfu" is a whole breast stuffed with spinach and feta, juicy, fragrant, topped with a creamy wine sauce. Fresh rice with a just-steamed texture and good vegetables complete the plate.

The house baklava is authentically, tooth-achingly sweet, nutty and fresh.

Come on a Friday or Saturday night and there's live "bouzouki" music.

THEO'S
911 Richmond Rd. (at Woodroffe)
(613) 728-0909
www.theosgreektaverna.com
Access: Fully accessible
Price: Main dishes $11.95 to $23.95
Open: Lunch Mon.-Sat.; dinner daily

TRATTORIA SPIGA

★★★ ½   Italian – Portuguese $$$

On the sleek black awning there's a new name. "Trattoria" Spiga, this place is now called, a subtle change from the original "Café" prefix. There are funky new lights, a bolder, more vibrant paint job, and some updated furnishings. And on the stairs that descend to the loos, a large peeping window has been added, for a view of Spiga's impressive wine cellar.

But when it comes to the cooking, this trattoria's gone back to its roots. A sizable chunk of the once all-Italian menu now reflects the Portuguese heritage of longtime co-owner and chef Joao Botelho.

Caldo verde, considered Portugal's national soup, fronts the menu. And interspersed with the pastas and risottos and veal parmigianas is a handful of classic Portuguese dishes — caldeirada de peixe (fish stew), carne alentejana (pork with clams), and three recipes (there are reportedly 362 others) featuring bacalhaus — salt cod. Fresh fish from Portuguese waters is a daily feature at the new Spiga.

It seems to me the cooking here is better than ever. All starters are winners: the caldo verde is rich chicken stock plump with potato, collard greens, and coriander, the whole well-seasoned with garlic and spicy chouriço. Chewy nuggets of grilled octopus are slick with garlic-rich oil, scattered with parsley, served with pickled vegetables; cod cakes are full-flavoured comfort food; stickleback are floured, fired up, fried, and addictive.

There are a dozen pasta offerings. A simple winner is the al dente linguine moistened with virgin oil, green with parsley, and pungent with garlic. On these wet, fragrant noodles is set a generous number of fresh clams, just-steamed. Want something richer? The gnocchi are delicious, bathed in a fragrant, wine-splashed tomato sauce. Richer still? Opt for those potato dumplings in the Gorgonzola sauce, sweet with leeks, rosy with roasted peppers, and of considerable cheese richness and bite.

Fresh fish is a Spiga strength. A showy whole fish called sargo (dorade, or white bream) is floured and fried, its white flesh soft and pliant beneath its crisp brown skin, sour with vinegar, aromatic with saffron and fennel, and sweetly pungent with roasted red pepper and lots and lots of wonderful garlic.

"Bacalhau a casa" is properly soaked of its saltiness; thick chunks of it arrive bathed in an oily broth within a ceramic roof tile, surrounded with potato, garlic, onions, and parsley. If you like salt cod, you will like this. There is also wild salmon from B.C. and Alaskan cod, both a steal at $19.

As for meat, there are the usual half-dozen veal dishes: marsala, picata, parmigiana — and osso bucco, the veal falling-off-the-shank tender, festooned with lemon rind, parsley, and garlic and served properly with a risotto Milanese, intensely aromatic with saffron. Back to Portugal for a taste of the classic — but wildly odd — pairing of pork with clams. Carne alentejana features well-marinated, tender chunks of pork tenderloin with whole steamed clams and masses of roast potatoes.

For dessert, there's delicious Portuguese rice pudding, and bread pudding — the latter a dense wedge made with coconut, almonds, and pine nuts, and a bittersweet maple sauce drizzled overtop.

There is so much here to recommend. But I do find the weak link is the service. And that isn't new. What's missing at Spiga is the hospitality factor. A dose of graciousness needs to be added to this otherwise very compelling restaurant.

The wine list remains a strength—particularly strong in the area of Spanish, Portuguese, and Italian reds—and the price of a dinner at Spiga remains very fair indeed.

TRATTORIA SPIGA

271 Dalhousie St. (at Murray)
(613) 241-4381
www.cafespiga.ca
Access: Step at entrance; washrooms are downstairs
Price: Pasta, risotto, and main dishes $11 to $25
Open: Lunch Mon.-Fri.; dinner daily

TRATTORIA ZINGARO

★★★ ½   Italian $$$

At the risk of perpetuating the stereotype of gypsies as colourfully clad, free-spirited wanderers, let me say that Michael Cumming's restaurant is aptly named. "Zingaro" means "gypsy," and this one pulses with colour and neighbourly spirit.

But appearances are where the likeness ends, for this zingaro stays put. Since 1996, Trattoria Zingaro has been firmly perched on its busy New Edinburgh corner, attracting the community with its consistently good food and welcoming atmosphere.

Let others go minimalist and taupe. Cumming's trattoria is a merriness of bold, playroom colours—plastered on walls, chairs, tables, even in his spotlights. His plates, too, are charged with colour as well as with the confident flavours of Tuscan cooking.

The menu leans heavily, almost exclusively, in fishy directions. There are always mussels—steamed on tonight's menu, in a tomato broth flooded with softly-cooked fennel, leeks, and portobello mushrooms, sweetened with roasted garlic. Crusty bread sops up the sauce. The antipasto platter is splendid and generous: house-smoked salmon wrapped around a herbed mascarpone cheese filling; a moist wedge of roasted vegetable frittata; an oil-slicked, well-garlicked purée of Romano beans; slices of Italian prosciutto; a lively tapenade; marinated Bocconcini; roasted red peppers; pickled beets; briny olives; artichokes; fruit. It is meant to be shared.

There are few restaurants in which I am guaranteed a carefully made risotto. Zingaro's is one of them. You can taste the wine, the saffron, the rich stock in each plump, creamy, chewy grain of coddled rice. Sweet sea scallops, big clams, crunchy shrimp, and grilled squid crown the moist mound. Mussels rim the bowl.

Tilapia, marlin, and salmon are the day's "three fish, three ways," each sauced separately, each cooked perfectly, presented on splendid mashed potatoes and furnished with a bonanza of perfect vegetables — pickled beets, roasted parsnips, beans, bok choy, carrots, peppers, squash, and brussels sprouts.

The highlight of the meat dishes is a slow-roasted chicken. Always a test of a kitchen, this bird passes with honours: the flesh so moist, so melting; the skin crisp, salty; the flavours rich.

Cumming's desserts are the work of a gifted hand: a gossamer crème brûlée flavoured lightly with maple syrup, and a magnificent tiramisu with layers of rich mascarpone custard within a fresh, light, well-soused cake.

The wine list is mostly Italian and offers many options by the glass.

TRATTORIA ZINGARO
18 Beechwood Ave. (at Charlevoix)
(613) 744-6509
Access: Fully accessible
Price: Main dishes $10 to $22
Open: Lunch Mon.-Fri.; dinner daily

URBAN PEAR

★ ★ ★ ½   Contemporary $$$$

Ben Baird and Summer Lichty are the pair behind the Pear. Both are graduates of the Stratford Chefs School, with experience at Rundles Restaurant in Stratford and the Sooke Harbour House in British Columbia. The Urban Pear is their first restaurant.

It's a hugely impressive beginning.

A small room, long and narrow, with twenty pale wood tables snugly spaced on the bleached pine floors. The walls are tall and pistachio-coloured, with stylish copper accents. One wall is taken up by a long wooden bench with pillow paddings (thank you). The other wall is all window. It means lots of light floods this place. It also means a view of parked cars in the side lot. Privacy blinds help. One visit, arresting black-and-white photos adorn the walls. At the next, the lush, vibrant art of Maureen Ballagh changes the tone of the room entirely.

And, here and there, the pear: in a cup of posies, in a painting on the wall, in the shape of the pepper mills on the tables, and on the oversized white plates of remarkable food.

The menu is short and changes daily. One visit we begin with a carrot soup scented with coriander; on another, roasted beet with dill. Both are superb. A starter of grilled scallops, sweet-fleshed and perfectly supple, is paired with a sprightly pea-shoot salad, draped with oranges and roasted sunflower seeds. On a second night, in one of their signature big bowls, sea scallops again, floating in a broth scented with cucumber, streaked with carrot julienne, and settled with couscous.

An antipasti plate is notable for the room-temperature cheese of just the right runniness, the magnificent wrinkled Moroccan olives, sharp with chillies and garlic, and the perfectly ripe pears.

Main dishes bring us beef, supple and abundantly flavoured, the sweet onion–infused demi-glace rich with depth rather than heaviness. It comes with a divine wild-mushroom risotto and some early fall offerings: grilled radicchio, golden beets, and a mound of grilled and grated zucchini. We tuck into duck—melting flesh and bronzed skin—with potato röstis and wilted beet greens. And then a fillet of fresh perch with baby bok choy, baby potatoes, and astringent red cabbage in a sauce scented with sesame and fragrant with carrot.

A month later, a new menu offers us braised rabbit (a meaty leg and a soft breast cooked on a skewer of rosemary) with roasted potatoes, spring onions, mini-squash, and pears perfumed with lemon and thyme. There is duck again, this time the breast, rimmed with just the right layer of fat for flavour, the skin crisp, the flesh rare, positioned on a ring of beet settled atop a mound of pink chard, wrapped in a sauce of reduced duck juices. It comes with a ground-duck and roasted-pear terrine wrapped in puff pastry. Wonderful stuff.

An Urban Pear lunch begins with a splendid bowl of noodles, dotted with a fresh assembly of vegetables: meaty shiitake mushrooms, strips of carrot, zucchini, onion, celery, bok choy, and pea pods, all of it in a sesame-scented broth, topped with a slab of crusty-grilled red snapper.

I find that the so-called trifle is missing the true richness of custard and cake, and I am not convinced stuffing a peach with white chocolate and wrapping it with phyllo entirely works. But the white chocolate and rhubarb bavarois (served with a rhubarb sorbet) is lovely.

Lately, I've dropped in for a chocolate fix and found it immensely well sated by a dense, dark, almost-too-bitter rectangle of Belgium's finest, drizzled sweetly (thankfully) with caramel, and served with crème fraîche and a puddle of roasted crabapple coulis.

Half the wine list is given over to Canadian entries.

URBAN PEAR
151 Second Ave. (at Bank)
(613) 569-9305
Access: Fully accessible
Price: Main dishes $22 to $30
Open: Brunch/lunch Sun.-Fri.; dinner daily

VERANDA D'OR

★★   Chinese $

You find Veranda d'Or on the east side of Conroy Road at Lorry Greenberg Drive, in the corner of a strip mall. Inside the big room, all is pink and red — tables, chairs, curtains, everything. Even the menu is framed in red, with almost half of the hundred-plus dishes on offer marked with a wee red heart, sweetly flagging the "lively" dishes.

Veranda d'Or concentrates on the cooking of China's largest province, Szechwan, where the weather is colder and the spices hotter.

Fried wontons have flavour and spice enough to wake up the palate, straighten the back, and get you ready to eat more. "Kou-tieh" are yummy dumplings filled with seasoned minced pork, steamed, and then fried on one side. The spring rolls are stuffed with the usual shredded vegetables and are not particularly memorable, but they improve when the homemade tamarind sauce is applied to them. Slippery noodle casings enclose firm nuggets of a tasty pork forcemeat in the house wonton soup, the broth heady with the pungent-aromatic five-spice powder. There are sticky-crisp chicken wings and aromatic moo shu pork with paper-thin pancakes.

Top marks to the sea bass. It is served whole, impeccably cooked, in a pool of sauce that is at once dark, smooth, oily, fiery hot, and slightly sweet, dotted innocently with scallion. Sea scallops are luscious. They taste fresh, sizzling on a platter with peppers, onions, and tomato, the texture of this pretty dish appealing with the softness of fish and the crunch of vegetable, all of it slipping down very well. Lemon chicken is the usual deep-fried standard, the meat within its puffy casing moist, and the lemon flavour significant. General Tao's chicken is not the sickly-sweet version you encounter in many Chinese restaurants. Here it is a platter of tender chicken in an intensely flavoured sauce, heady of ginger, soy, and garlic, and powerfully hot with the dried red peppers scattered among its other elements. Last two hits: shrimp are paired with crackling wisps of deep-fried spinach, and tender strips of beef are set in a spicy-hot, sesame-seeded, highly aromatic sauce, toned down with as much steamed rice as two chopsticks will allow.

Battered-up mashed bananas, deep-fried and glazed with honey and sesame, are dessert. They are too sweet for me. Bagged up, they go cold the next day in the lads' lunches. Big hit.

VERANDA D'OR
4 Lorry Greenberg Dr. (at Conroy)
(613) 736-1965
Access: Restaurant is accessible; washrooms are small
Price: Main dishes $9.95 to $14.95
Open: Lunch Mon.-Fri.; dinner daily

VIETNAMESE KITCHEN

★★   **Vietnamese** $

As my twelve-year-old hurtles out of childhood, what was once the straightforward task of finding him a new winter jacket is now charged with stress. After an unsuccessful hour at yet another sports store, we shuffle to the restaurant next door: a warm welcome, a pot of hot tea, a cold Hue beer and steaming bowls of pho. There is nothing more restorative.

It's a very yellow, very plain room, owned by a very kind family. Its menu is not unlike every other Vietnamese menu—long and repetitive—except for the sizable section of Szechwan dishes. How I long for a Vietnamese restaurant to give me a dozen choices and no more. Especially after exposure to some two hundred parkas.

I tend to order what I always order, particularly with my family. We know what we like, and we like what we get here. Perfectly balanced sweet and sour soup; Vietnamese spring rolls packed with flavour; fresh rice paper rolls stuffed with mint, basil, honey-marinated pork, lettuce, and noodle. The crispy quails are still moist inside, their deep-fried skin crackling. A wrap-and-roll platter of barbecued pork is tender meat backed up with soft noodles, crisp lettuce, sweet and sour vegetables, and sparkling herbs.

A good stock is the solid foundation for a bowl of pho, or beef noodle soup; lime juice and fish sauce balance the sweetness. You add hot sauce if you wish, bean sprouts, herbs, and begin the delicious journey through the entire bowl—no mean feat, but a pleasant one.

From the Szechwan section, I order eggplant with chicken, sizzling with black bean sauce. (This I eat, largely and happily, by myself.)

They have Hue beer here. The kids like the fruit shakes. I like the lemongrass tea, the service, the no-frills décor, and the remarkably reasonable bill.

VIETNAMESE KITCHEN
478 Bank St. (near Gladstone)
(613) 593-8991
www.vietnamesekitchen.com
Access: Two steps into restaurant; washroom is small
Price: Main dishes $5.95 to $13.95
Open: Lunch Mon.-Sat.; dinner daily

VIETNAM PALACE

★★ ½   Vietnamese $

The ritual of sharing food from communal platters is one of the great pleasures of a Vietnamese meal. So are the flavours created by the raw materials: chilli, lime juice, vinegar, mint, basil, curry, lemongrass, and nuoc mam, a condiment made from fermented anchovies and used in Vietnamese cooking as readily as soy sauce is used in Chinese.

But more than these palate-waking ingredients is the fun of creating individual mouthfuls. Each one can contrast with the one before, as you mix and match the materials in different ways, rolling and dipping the bites into various dishes of sweet or pungent or spicy sauces. It creates a whole mosaic of flavours.

At the Vietnam Palace, the spring rolls are satisfying, the deep-fried squid is better, and the crispy quail, with its pungent, potent lemongrass sauce, is best of all. Wrap-and-roll platters can feature tough meat. Next visit, it's tender again. Rather depends on your luck. Thin slices of rare sirloin are still rare, but cooking fast in the basin of aromatic beef broth. There are noodles in this bowl, onion too. We add mint, basil, bean sprouts, a splash more fish sauce.

The fish highlights include scallops sautéed with lemongrass and hot chillies, shrimp stir-fried with fresh pineapple, and a moist, yielding hunk of sea bass, pungent with ginger and black bean sauce.

There is a sizable vegetarian section on this menu, with all the usual absurdity of mock chicken and mock eel (read: tofu). We had the papaya salad and the fried bean curd with tomato sauce, both good.

Unless you're a fan of Vietnamese desserts, better stick with tea.

VIETNAM PALACE

819 Somerset St. West (between Booth and Rochester)
(613) 238-6758
Access: Stairs at entrance; washrooms are on second floor
Price: Main dishes $5.25 to $18.95
Open: Lunch and dinner daily

VILLAGE CAFÉ

★ ★ ½   Eclectic $$

In a long, narrow space of bronzed walls, oval mirrors, and re-
volving art, there is seating for about forty on mismatched chairs
at whimsically stencilled tables. A rack is full of newspapers and
magazines. You can take a sunny seat by the front window with
the local rag, or perch on one of the half-dozen stools at the bar.
At the back, where another dozen tables afford a view of the open
kitchen, the dining is darker, slightly more intimate.

This is a reliably busy place; a neighbourhood restaurant of eclectic
leanings, casual, affordable, cheery. The dinner menu is primarily
Mediterranean (spanakopita, hummus, pasta dishes with southern
flavours) with a nod to Asia (salad rolls, coconut shrimp, tandoori
salmon).

At noon, the Village Café offers soups, sandwiches, and salads.
A sweet potato purée, perfumed with rosemary, is followed by a
smoked turkey sandwich on thick sourdough, fragrant of basil,
sun-dried tomato, and an olive tapenade. It makes a heck of a
lunch for $12. You can be clever and pair the day's Thai peanut
soup (splashed with coconut milk) with foccacia-filled slices of
Szechwan-marinated chicken, moistened with a curry mayo. With
the sandwiches come balsamic-dressed greens prettied with long
strands of carrot. Or, for $1.50 more, you can have the reliably good
house Caesar.

A fragrant dipping sauce of orange and sesame oil is provided for
the fresh spring rolls, which are plump with soft chicken, thin vege-
tables, and noodles scented with pickled ginger. Thick, flavourful
crab cakes arrive on spinach, with a black-bean and corn salsa. Globs
of rich goat cheese and balsamic-fried mushrooms top a plate of

mixed leaves. The spinach salad is a mound of the dark young greens dotted with toasted pecans and grilled bacon, dressed comfortably with a warm honey-mustard vinaigrette.

The list of mains begins with a vegetarian risotto ($15) and ends with a full rack of New Zealand lamb ($30). We look to the middle of the list, choosing the salmon and one of the three pasta dishes offered. Rubbed and reddened with Indian spices, the fish is fresh, cooked well (meaning not long), and topped with a mango chutney piqued with cinnamon, raisins, onion, and peppers. Tuscan flavours shine in a plate of linguine, the noodles treated with garlic oil, sun-dried tomato, prosciutto, and balsamic-splashed mushrooms.

The desserts are brought in from the Ritz bakery, and their pedigree shows. I find the white chocolate cranberry tart painfully sweet, but the chocolate cheesecake is wonderful, as is the five-fruit crumble.

The Village "cellar" is a short list of pretty ordinary offerings, with every one (yes!) of the two dozen wines available by the glass or half-litre.

VILLAGE CAFÉ
295 Richmond Rd. (east of Churchill)
(613) 728-2162
www.thevillagecafe.net
Access: One small step into restaurant; washrooms are small but on main level
Price: Main dishes $15 to $30
Open: Lunch and dinner Mon.-Sat.; brunch Sun.; closed Sun. dinner

WASABI

★★ ½   Japanese $$

Wasabi is a New York chain of five restaurants spread throughout the neighbourhoods of Brooklyn and Queens. This Byward Market Wasabi makes six. You may wonder, why Ottawa? Indeed. Must be because this town is all a-twitter with the pleasure of raw fish. Or, if we're not twittering yet, perhaps it's time we were.

Whatever the thinking that settled on our town for this sushi joint, we are blessed with it.

A window waterfall greets you as you enter, jazz music plays. The look is smart, clean, and understated. And the raw goods are the familiar favourites — tuna, salmon, yellowtail — plus seasonal items, like toro (tuna belly), mirugai (giant clam), and hotatei (live scallop). I'm working on acquiring a taste for uni — sea urchin — a fleshy, flabby creature with a powerful oceanic flavour and, for me, a bit of work. Wasabi is a good place to experiment with the raw and the flabby. The stuff won't break the budget.

Not a raw fish fan? The tataki dishes, for $9.95, present you with a generous rectangle of sushi-grade tuna, seared on the outside, gloriously rare on the inside, sliced and fanned and served with very fine rice.

Even that much red is too much? There is tempura: fresh shrimp with all the right snap and crackle are dipped in a light, wispy batter along with some big branches of broccoli, both perfectly cooked. You can start with miso soup or the chukai salad of seaweed and diced cucumber in a rousing vinaigrette. Young watercress is steamed until just-wilted and doused with ginger, garlic, and sesame oil. There are good gyoza (meat and vegetable pot stickers) and chicken kara-age, battered and deep-fried chunks of tender chicken, tasty, sticky, served with a ginger sauce.

The hotatei masago is a hot dish of scallops and supposedly wild mushrooms in a cream and roe sauce, all broiled in a scallop shell. Fine, except that the mushrooms are decidedly tame. And another disappointment: tough, dry chicken teriyaki in a lacklustre sauce, with undercooked, bland vegetables.

Wasabi offers four choices of sake, Japanese beer, and a wine list they've attempted to match with the menu. Every bottle is available by the glass.

WASABI
41 Clarence St. (close to Sussex)
(613) 241-3636
Access: Easy access through the mall entrance; two steps to washrooms in restaurant, but public washrooms in mall are close and fully accessible
Price: Sushi à la carte $2 to $3.25 per item; main dishes $12.95 to $15.95
Open: Lunch and dinner daily

WILFRID'S

★★★   Canadian $$$$

A $1.2 million overhaul has Wilfrid's looking pretty darn good. (Yes, I know, so would we all.) The high-windowed dining room of the Château Laurier continues to afford a fine view of the Hill and the Canal, but gone is the strict formality of the place. Muted shades of beige are splashed with striking bits of blue. Contemporary fittings grant the room a more come-as-you-are feel. Window tables are still the choice ones, but the terraced arrangement of the room's levels provides pretty good scenery from just about anywhere.

Two things have not changed: the service continues to be a sharp cut above; and the commitment remains to Canadian and seasonal content on the menu and wine list.

By hotel dining room standards, the dinner menu is blessedly short. There are subtle Asian imprints on some of the dishes—the Miramichi Bay lobster salad is treated with a rice wine and cilantro vinaigrette, the Brome Lake duck is sweetly glazed with soy, ginger and port. But the spring menu is mostly an ode to Ontario lamb and Newfoundland crab, Atlantic salmon and Nunavut caribou, prepared with local strengths: asparagus, wild blueberries, Québec goat cheese, and Ottawa Valley honey.

The lunch buffet is an attractive presentation of a manageable number of dishes: lettuces are presented in large, linen-wrapped baskets. Dressings taste homemade. A wild game and pistachio terrine has good gamey flavour. There is fresh halibut, moist, lightly sauced, and pork loin, roasted to pink, served with a full-flavoured jus. There are roasted vegetables, done right. Yes, there are disappointments: the spinach agnolotti is stuffed with a nondescript, tasteless filling, and the fish terrine is on the gelatinous side. But all in all, as buffets go, this is a reliably good one.

À la carte, the seafood chowder boasts perfect fish: soft salmon, mussels, scallops, and shrimp with potato and carrot in a cream-splashed, comforting broth. A salad niçoise has all the classic elements: onion, olives, potato, haricots verts, and then (hurrah!), a thick, juicy steak of fresh tuna, pepper-crusted, grilled to medium-rare. Some starters misfire slightly: the lobster consommé has good lobster flavour, and the scallop within the dark, clear broth is quite perfect, but the broth is two pinches too salty. Same error with the chicken: juicy and tender, served with a sweet onion marmalade and a tasty entourage of fingerling potatoes, but still, still, the bird is uncomfortably salty. A gentler touch with the surface salt is needed here.

There is caribou on this menu, a thick double chop, roasted to rare, set in a puddle of deglazed pan juices made crimson with beet. It comes with roasted carrots and an uncomfortably rich barley "stew," cooked risotto-style (only with too much cream)—the plump grains dotted with sun-dried blueberries. And there is salmon, of course: a thick square of the succulent fish, upon which an enormous grilled shrimp and perfect scallop rest. The collection is sauced with an impeccable butter sauce, fragrant with dill, dotted with a tiny dice of root vegetables and zucchini.

The dessert buffet is an attractive display of complex sweets, most of which taste of quality ingredients.

Wilfrid's wine list is vast and a showcase of our country's great wineries.

WILFRID'S
Fairmont Château Laurier Hotel
1 Rideau St. (at Mackenzie)
(613) 562-7043
www.fairmont.com
Access: Fully wheelchair accessible
Price: Main dishes $19 to $38
Open: Daily

ZIBIBBO

★★½   Italian $$

The walls are a cornucopia of colour and textures: interlocking teak on one, seaweed on another, cork along the bar, camouflage green everywhere else. The lights are pillowy, clouded, curved to fit the room. The crowd seems young, sleek, there either to eat on the main level or to head to "TheCamarilloBrilloUpstairs," a pocket-size DJ lounge where there are martinis, music, and (on our night), an in-house artist spreading orange paint on an enormous white canvas.

Zibibbo (subtitle: Italian Soul Kitchen) is run by the team of Luigi Meliambro and Carmine Bucciarelli. The food is homespun Italian, rustic and unpretentious, and tastes of quality ingredients handled with talent and care.

We start with succulent quail, bronzed and juicy, paired with smoky-grilled eggplant, arranged on a citrus-dressed mound of baby spinach sweetened with pomegranate syrup. Ye olde deep-fried zucchini sticks are updated into fritters, the grated green bound with potato, fragrant with basil, and sharp with a grating of Grana cheese. A Caesar salad is memorable for the accompanying anchovy-drenched bread.

Salty-good pancetta is skewered with chunks of marinated lamb, treated with a paste of parsley, garlic, capers, anchovies, and bread-crumbs, moistened with oil, grilled perfectly and served with a lentil salad. Tagliatelle noodles, flecked with mint, provide the foundation for a braised lamb stew, fragrant with basil.

A veal chop is fat, seared on the outside, welcomingly pink and moist within. It is topped with a sage-scented braise of pancetta, onion, shiitake and portobello mushrooms, all of it piled on a mound of bitter greens dripping-rich with pan juices. This is perhaps the best of the mains. But we are also drawn to the heady saffron smells in a seafood stew, where mussels, clams, scallops, crawfish, ocean perch, and shavings of fennel swim in a well-scented tomato-based broth, grounded with couscous. Rabbit is stewed in white wine, the skin bronzed, the meat soft, yielding, sweetened with caramelized onion, spiked with orange zest and served with wilted spinach, lentils, and carrots. Cornmeal-coated monkfish is drenched in garlic, pepper, and oil, sweet with raisins, served with dynamite roasted potatoes, roasted sweet peppers, rapini, and caperberries. There is lots happening on these Zibibbo plates, but the ingredients all hang together, their flavours blending, the results tasty.

The texture of a hazelnut chocolate brownie is not quite on; too liquid in some parts, too crusty in others. Better the house panna cotta, a gelatin-molded classic Italian dessert of cream (panna) and sugar, here served with apricots softened in a cardamom-infused sugar syrup. The house cheesecake is rich, dense, with a pleasing, gentle flavour, and cannoli (Sicilian fried pastry tubes) are filled with pistachio-studded, orange-scented ricotta cream, finished with a dusting of sugar, and united with a blob of fantastic pistachio ice cream.

"Zibibbo" is the name of a white grape from Sicily. The restaurant offers an all-Italian wine list, with the exception of three VQA listings. All are available by the bottle, the glass, and the quartino.

ZIBIBBO
495 Somerset St. West (at Lyon)
(613) 233-0821
www.zibibbo.org
Access: Two steps into restaurant; washrooms are upstairs
Price: Main dishes $13 to $25
Open: Lunch Tues.-Fri.; dinner Tues.-Sun.; closed Mon.

LISTINGS

Cuisine Type

Neighbourhood Index

FULLY ACCESSIBLE

Wine Lists Worth Noting